WILDLIFE WATCHER'S HANDBOOK

FRANK T. HANENKRAT

WILDLIFE WATCHER'S HANDBOOK

WINCHESTER PRESS

Library of Congress Cataloging in Publication Data

Hanenkrat, Frank T
  Wildlife watcher's handbook.

  Bibliography: p.
  Includes index.
  1. Wildlife watching. I. Title.
QL60.H36   591   77-23565
ISBN 0-87691-245-5

Printed in the United States of America

Published by Winchester Press
205 East 42nd Street
New York, N.Y. 10017

TO MY FATHER,
WHO TAUGHT ME TO LOVE THE OUTDOORS

SEMANTICS

In this book, *he* is used to refer to human beings of either sex, merely to avoid repeatedly writing *he or she*. I hope this device will not be taken amiss.

ACKNOWLEDGMENTS

I am especially indebted to George Peper, formerly an editor at Winchester Press, for making the initial suggestion that led to the writing of this book; and to the following individuals who had the patience to help in significant ways, either by answering numerous questions, providing references, making suggestions, contributing observations, or reading and correcting parts or all of the manuscript: Dr. James Carico, Dr. Ruskin Freer, William Frank Hanenkrat, Elaine Kibbe, Myriam P. Moore, Dr. Gwynn Ramsey, Dr. Shirley Rosser, and Shirley Whitt. I am grateful to Jacqueline Asbury, William Frank Hanenkrat, and Thelma Twery for assistance in preparing the illustrations.

CONTENTS

INTRODUCTION

People have many reasons for wanting to approach and observe wild animals in their natural surroundings. Hunters, of course, have sought to do this since the dawn of man's appearance on earth, but recently a phenomenal growth has taken place in the numbers of people who wish to do so for other reasons. Among these are birders, ecologists, biologists, photographers, ethologists, writers, artists, wildlife management personnel, and many others who have interests, personal or professional, in wildlife. This book is written for all of them. It discusses a number of techniques that have proved successful through the years and examines some of the most recent findings about bird and mammal behavior.

Most people find the sight of a wild animal exciting and pleasant. We may speculate that this response is a product of our often overlooked heritage. In the past few centuries—a very brief time in the scheme of evolution—we humans have created cultural systems based upon technology and have, in a sense, put ourselves in conflict with nature. But during a past that extends back through 3,500,000 years, we seem to have lived in harmony with it. For much of that enormous time span, early man lived not only in harmony with nature, but in awe of it. Our ancestors worshiped many manifestations of nature's power—the sun, rivers, flowers, trees, and an astounding variety of animals, including birds, mammals, reptiles, fish, and members of other classes as well. Careful study shows that a central tenet in nature cults is the belief that the well-being of the worshipers depends upon the goodwill of the object or animal being worshiped; and that this goodwill must be earned through demonstrations of veneration, respect, and gratitude.

Ironically, we have come to realize that in a very real way our well-being does indeed depend on our having respect and veneration for other forms of life. We have learned this through blunders of near-catastrophic proportions. Only a few years ago, it was fashionable to proclaim that technological progress could make us self-sufficient and completely independent of nature. This "progressive" view fostered an attitude of superiority toward wild creatures: they existed only to be ignored, exploited, or exterminated.

Yet even at the height of the phase when veneration of nature was replaced by veneration of technology, our living habits belied our professed superiority to and independence from other forms of life. In evolving out of the world of nature we apparently brought with us a deep longing for contact with other species, a longing that shows itself in our continuing and almost fanatical attachment to household pets. Contact with other species clearly satisfies some deep needs. Why else would millions of technological Americans bestow loving, often expensive attention on creatures who perform absolutely no "practical" function?

Considering this matter, one of the great students of animal and human behavior of our time, the scientist Konrad Lorenz, in *King Solomon's Ring*, has written about why men keep dogs:

In these days, the value of a dog to man is purely a psychological one. . . . The pleasure which I derive from my dog . . . seems like a re-establishment of the immediate bond with that unconscious omniscience that we call nature. The price which man had to pay for his culture and civilization was the severing of this bond which had to be torn to give him specific freedom of will. But our infinite longing for paradise lost is nothing else than a half-conscious yearning for our ruptured ties.

The longing for these "ruptured ties" is something almost everyone feels now and then. Perhaps it explains why so many Americans are seeking to renew their contacts with the woods and fields. Most of them seem to agree that time spent in communion with nature is deeply satisfying. And significantly, the majority of people who are seeking this renewed communion are well educated, aware, and sensitive to environmental issues. Many are reading and studying and then going out and observing firsthand the intimate relationships between animals and their surroundings. They are discovering that a swamp or a field or a woods that formerly seemed only undeveloped land is in fact a precious, perhaps irreplaceable home for wild creatures that they can relate to on a meaningful personal basis. Many acquire a painful awareness that unless human expansion and pollution are restrained, more and more wild creatures will disappear from the earth forever. Contemplating the extinction of a species produces vague sensations of longing and loneliness and reveals that in the recesses of our human nature exists the capacity for real love of other species—our fellow voyagers on what some have called Spaceship Earth.

The thin, fragile zone of life on the surface of our planet—thinner relatively than the skin of an apple—is threatened now by so many technological insults that it must be carefully monitored to prevent catastrophe. One of the best ways to do so is to keep a careful watch on animal populations. How this works can be illustrated by a familiar analogy. Coal miners used to keep a caged canary with them in the mine shafts. If poisonous but undetectable gases began to collect in the shafts, the canary, being more sensitive to the poison, would die from the toxins and provide the miners with a sufficiently early warning to enable them to escape. The same principle operates in the outdoors, where wild-animal populations often give advance warnings of accumulating poisons. The dramatic decline of peregrine falcons, brown pelicans, and other birds in response to DDT and other pollutants is a vivid example of how wild creatures serve as indicators to help us safeguard the earth from unintentional disaster. As scientists are fond of pointing out, we don't know which living species may give us our next early warning, which may be crucial. For our own well-being, then, we need to protect all living things and exist in harmony with them. To do this, we need to know how their populations are faring.

Large-scale population monitoring is conducted annually on many species, with most of the fieldwork being done by amateurs. Their observations about different species are channeled into various data banks, such as one maintained by the U.S. Fish and Wildlife Service in Laurel, Md. There computers store millions of pieces of data on each species' yearly abundance, migration activities, range changes, and other factors of population dynamics. The overall picture that emerges from these constantly updated data banks provides invaluable insights into what is happening in the environment. This data-gathering and analyzing process relies heavily on hunters and birders as the major amateur contributors.

Since the advent of modern game-management techniques, hunting has become controlled and regulated in such a way as to maintain, and in many cases increase, the populations of game birds and mammals. Today in the United States, the great threat to endangered species is not hunting pressure, but rather the loss of suitable living space. The business mentality that desires to "develop" wildlands is a constant, unremitting threat, and hunters have been a powerful force in generating political pressure to restrain development and to create protected public wildlands, including breeding grounds, wintering grounds, and refuges where various species are assured of finding the correct habitat to meet their special requirements. Hunters also generate the funds necessary to manage these areas. Revenues from the sale of state and federal hunting permits and from taxes on firearms and ammunition support

Through license fees and taxes upon hunting equipment, hunters finance wildlife management programs on both state and federal levels. Since most of these programs center on habitat management, they are of benefit not only to game species, but to nongame species as well.

the managers, biologists, and regulatory officers who man these areas. Hunters also founded and give financial support to such sportsmen's groups as Ducks Unlimited and other organizations that have created important private refuge systems to augment the public ones. As a result of these efforts, often international in scope, many species have been saved from almost certain extinction and are now thriving—as, indeed, are most game animals and birds that have adequate living conditions. That responsible hunters have been so powerfully instrumental in these efforts is often overlooked; they deserve recognition for their accomplishments.

In addition, hunters perform an important monitoring function on game populations. A group of hunters can provide much more thorough coverage of an area than the limited number of wildlife biologists could ever hope to attain by themselves. Hunters register their kills of monitored species at check stations, enabling biologists to determine a species' abundance and to examine the kills for evidence of disease, malnutrition, breeding condition, and other information. Hunters also return to a central clearing house the bands placed on migratory game birds by the U.S. Fish and Wildlife Service, thus providing data on species' migration habits and population changes. The insights that emerge from an analysis of these kinds of data enable wildlife management personnel to adjust hunting regulations and management techniques to ensure that an optimum population of each species is preserved for the future.

The second, and larger, group of amateurs who contribute to wildlife monitoring is made up of birders. Birdwatching, as the activity was once called, was at one time considered the mildly humorous diversion of a few eccentrics; but in the past decade or so, birding, as it is now called, has become one of the fastest-growing outdoor recreations. Today U.S. birders number close to 20 million and the number is growing rapidly.

Birders are such a varied group that to describe them adequately is almost impossible. At the lowest echelon are those who might maintain a winter bird feeder and enjoy the sight of birds, often without being able to identify the species they see. At the highest echelon are the dedicated members of the "600 Club" who attempt to see every one of the 645 or so species that nest in North America north of Mexico. These dedicated birders travel extensively and often go to great lengths in order to see a single rare species. They have a close-knit communications network and instantly inform one another of unusual sightings. In 1975, when a Ross's gull made a rare visit to New York, a corporate executive in California was on his way by chartered plane within an hour of the first reported sighting in order to add the bird to his "life list."

Obviously, most birders fall somewhere between these two extremes. A typical birder probably maintains a bird feeder in his yard and frequently birds in nearby areas, keeping some kind of informal record of what he sees. He probably plans weekend or vacation trips to see species that don't occur near his home. He probably belongs to a local bird club and aids the club's efforts in annual, organized bird-censusing activities.

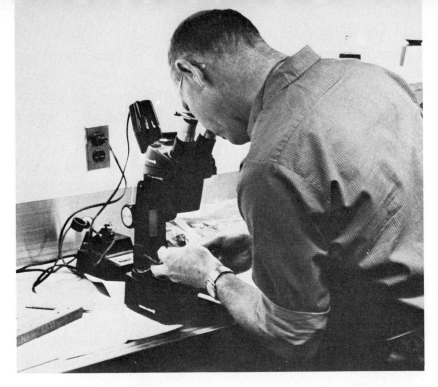

The Fish and Wildlife Service conducts many kinds of research. Here, Ellwood Martin, a laboratory technician, examines the crops of Virginia rails, supplied by hunters, for evidence of age, sex, and lead shot ingestion. Research such as this aids in the development of sound wildlife management programs.

Bird clubs, found in almost every major town and city throughout North America, participate in several kinds of nationally organized, seasonal censusing efforts. Their findings are carefully screened for accuracy at the local level, perhaps also at a regional level, and are then passed to a national clearing house where all the data are combined to produce a continent-wide picture of bird populations in the various annual seasons. The Audubon Society, the Hawk Migration Association of North America, and the U.S. Fish and Wildlife Service are among several national organizations that supervise these activities. The findings can be of enormous consequence. Birds are plentiful and relatively easy to see and identify; and because the many different species inhabit almost every niche of the environment and eat almost every kind of available food, any changes in environmental structure or accumulation of pollutants in the food chain are quickly reflected in species populations. The discovery of accumulating toxins as reflected in declining peregrine and pelican populations has already been mentioned; other instances could be cited. Thus an amateur birder can both enjoy a pleasant year-round outdoor hobby and at the same time contribute to important and necessary scientific research.

It should be emphasized, however, that the data-gathering value of pursuing wild animals is, to the participant, only incidental to his primary purpose, which is to enjoy the outdoors. A beginner, in fact, should not be concerned with data collecting at all. He should be concerned only with enjoying and learning about the animal or animals that interest him. As his knowledge and expertise increase, he will, as a matter of course, learn to recognize what is unusual or significant and will feel a natural desire to report such findings to someone in a position to make use of the data.

All of us who use the outdoors for work or recreation should observe certain ethical and legal restraints. Many of us forget, when caught up in our zeal for wild creatures, that they depend upon a complex ecosystem that rests upon a base of green plants. Destroy the balance or diversity of the plant life in an area and many animals will die off or disappear within hours, or a few days at most. This basic fact seems to acquire a red-letter urgency when we consider that each day in the United States, 2,000 acres of land are converted from rural to urban use; and that the Department of Interior's Office of Endangered Species has started action to place as many as 3,200 plants from all fifty states on the official endangered list, and has an additional 23,642 plant species under review for possible listing, making a total of more than 24,000 species of plants under study as possibly endangered.

Do not needlessly destroy vegetation. Above all, do not pick wild flowers or dig up wild plants unless the species is abundant over a large area, and then do so only sparingly. Leave plants to propagate and continue their gentle contributions to the ecosystem.

We should also remember that we have an ethical as well as legal obligation not to interfere with the lives of wild animals, except perhaps noxious insects and a few common pest species in other classes. Don't kill any wild mammal, bird, reptile, insect, spider, amphibian, fish, mollusk, or crustacean unless you are certain that current laws specifically permit you to do so and you have a valid reason for doing it. State and federal laws now govern the hunting of virtually every wild animal in

Chandler Robbins, senior author of the popular field guide Birds of North America *and Non-game Project Leader with the Fish and Wildlife Service, here discusses computer analysis of annual breeding bird surveys with Mrs. Myriam P. Moore.*

North America, prescribing hunting seasons and bag limits on game species and prohibiting the hunting of other species. State and federal laws also prohibit interfering with the breeding cycles of wild animals by molesting dens or nests or by disturbing the animals' parental behavior. Regulations also prohibit unlicensed poisoning, trapping, baiting, taming, transporting, selling, banding, marking, and even handling of most wild creatures. If uncertain of the laws, check with your local game warden or refuge manager.

All of us should also show voluntary restraint (and observance of law) by staying away from endangered or rare species. For many of us who are intensely interested in wildlife this amounts to a kind of self-denial, and perhaps we should be able to earn points in some way by *not* having made the trip to see a rare creature. Many of us would like to see California condors at their nests, or peregrines at their aeries, or, if one should be found, an active ivory-billed woodpecker's nest. Don't try. No amount of interest in or love for animals entitles anyone to disturb these or other dwindling species.

Many times it is easy to forget that the rewards of observation do not depend on finding a species that is rare or exotic or unusual. For example, a few years ago I became interested in birds of prey—specifically the hawks and owls of Virginia. I confidently began reading about them and studying them in the wild, thinking that I could become quite expert in two or three years. I read everything I could find; I made numerous observations in the wild. I rehabilitated two owls given me by a zoo and released them, by stages, back into the woods. I became interested in and took up falconry. I participated in spring and autumn censuses of raptors on the Blue Ridge and on the Virginia coast. I visited hawk trapping and banding stations. For an extensive period, I made almost daily observations of hawks and almost weekly observations of owls. And after about four years of study, I feel that I have only scratched the surface of what could be known about this fascinating group of birds. I do not cite this to flaunt my modesty; rather, to emphasize that almost any species of bird or mammal, even a familiar one, offers the opportunity for many years of study, pleasure, and enjoyment.

I

HOW WILD ANIMALS PERCEIVE THEIR WORLD

Compared to humans, wild birds and mammals are astonishingly alert and perceptive. If you and I walked through a natural area in the same way we walk down a street, all the wild animals there would detect our presence long before we detected theirs. Alertness and keen senses have far greater survival value among wild animals than among humans. We differ radically from almost all the rest of the animal kingdom in that we have evolved a complex social structure that enables us to care for a member of our species who has a handicap, such as poor vision, enabling him to survive and pass on his genetic defect to his offspring. But in the rest of the animal world this social support system rarely exists. Most birds and mammals beyond a certain age must fend for themselves, and the slow-witted and those with impaired senses quickly fall victim to starvation, injury, or predation. As a result of this constant evolutionary pressure toward improved genetic structure, healthy wild animals not only are strikingly alert, but also possess senses that are almost unbelievably keen. Birds and mammals possess either vision, or hearing, or a sense of smell—and sometimes all of these—that is much superior to ours. Wild animals are constantly wary of danger, and most have a strong fear of humans. Fortunately, though, there are measures you can take to conceal yourself from detection or to allay the animal's fear of your presence. Those measures will be discussed after we come to understand the unique ways by which animals perceive and structure their world.

The sense of vision

All wild birds and many wild mammals have far better vision than humans. In order to understand how and why they see better, we'll briefly review how the human eye works and use it as a standard. In very simple terms, the human eye is a sphere with an aperture in the front—the pupil—that controls the amount of light entering the eye. Also in the front is a lens, which focuses the incoming light rays to form an image on the rear of the eye, the retina. The lens controls the width of the field of view (about 150 degrees for each eye) and the distance of the point of focus. It may suffer from defects that produce astigmatism, nearsightedness, or farsightedness, conditions that can be corrected by eyeglasses or contact lenses. A normal or even a corrected lens can resolve images sufficiently well that an average person can see details of a figure subtending one minute of arc—the standard measuring device being the familiar eye chart in the doctor's office—and a person who can see these details is said to have 20/20 vision.

But the resolving power of the eye is not determined by the lens alone. Resolution limits are also imposed by the retina, which receives the image produced by the lens and relays the image to the brain. The retina consists of a mosaic of light-sensitive cells, each of which registers a tiny portion of the image and transmits signals about what it "sees." Because these cells are separated from one another, the parts of the image that fall between the cells are simply lost—they are never "seen" by cells—and so part of the image produced by the lens is never perceived. For this reason, no kind of eye-glass or contact lens can improve the eye's ability to resolve details of unmagnified images beyond a fixed, inborn limit. In a few people's eyes, which are otherwise normal, the spaces between the retinal cells are greater than ordinary, and these people have worse-than-average vision, say 20/30; in others, the cells are more closely spaced than ordinary, and these people may have better-than-average vision, say 20/10. The number and density of cells on the retina is one way in which many wild animals' eyes differ markedly from our own.

Another important feature of the human retina is the distribution of the types of cells it contains. There are two types: cones, which register images in color; and rods, which register images only in black, white, and shades of gray. In the human eye the greatest concentration of receptor cells is found in the area called the fovea, located near the center of the retina. This is the area that receives the image when we look directly at something, and because the cells in the fovea are densely packed and predominantly cones, they produce the clearest image and also provide the best color vision. Outside the fovea the cells are less densely packed and tend to contain a higher proportion of rods. Cones function well in bright light; but when the level of illumination falls, cones become less efficient until, below a certain threshold, they cease to function altogether. When we watch dusk approach, for instance, colors seem to fade as the cones become less efficient and the rods take over, rendering the world in terms of black, white, and gray. In light so dim that the cones have ceased entirely to function, if we want to see an object most clearly we have to look slightly to one side of it, allowing the image from the object to fall outside the fovea on an area of the retina containing a greater proportion of rods. But because the rods there are spaced widely apart, we cannot resolve the object very well. In short, we are fairly well adapted for daylight color vision, but poorly adapted for night vision.

Using the human eye as a standard, let's see how the vision

of other animals differs from ours. The eyes of all vertebrates operate in the same basic way, but often with surprising variations. Visual capability in animals can be determined by two kinds of scientific studies. One kind involves examining the physical structure of an animal's eyes. Using optical laws, an investigator can determine the width of visual field and the image-forming characteristics of an eye's lens, and the light-gathering capacities of the pupil. By examining the back of the eye he can determine the type and abundance of cells on the retina and get a good idea of its resolving power. The other way to study vision in animals is to observe their ability to see known quantities, either in the laboratory or in their normal environment. By combining the results of the two kinds of studies, investigators can get a crude idea of an animal's visual capacities. However, the conclusions must be regarded as approximations only, because some of the most important phases of the complex visual process take place in the neural relays between the eye and the brain and in the brain itself, where impulses from the eyes are integrated and structured. As yet, little is known about this aspect of vision, even among human subjects. It is possible that among different species, or even among individuals of the same species, the brain may process the incoming data in different ways. But though we are ignorant of much we would like to know about vision, studies so far have already yielded interesting results.

The sense of vision among birds

Let's start at the top, with hawks, who have the best vision known among any animals. A hawk's eyes—like those of most birds—are very large in proportion to body size. This is usually not apparent because the greater portion of all birds' eyes are concealed within their sockets. But a typical peregrine falcon, for instance, weighs less than two pounds, yet its eyes are almost as large as a human's. If a human had eyes of proportionate size, each would be several inches in diameter and weigh about one pound. The size of a hawk's eye makes pos-

*Hawks possess the keenest vision known among animals.
This young broad-winged hawk displays large, forward-
directed eyes that probably resolve more than eight times as
much detail as human eyes.*

sible great light-gathering power and a bright, clear image. Moreover, the density of retinal cells in many hawks is about eight times the density of retinal cells in a human eye (about 200,000 cells in the fovea of a human eye; about 1.5 million in the fovea of a hawk's eye). This alone suggests that a hawk should resolve about eight times more detail than we do—that it should see as much detail in a distant object, for example, as we could see through good-quality 8× binoculars. But a hawk's eye not only has a high retinal-cell count, it also has a small degree of magnifying power; the fovea has convex sides which enlarge a portion of the image and do so, in some cases, by as much as 30 percent.

Hawks and other birds also have superior neural connections between the retinal cells and the brain. In humans, for instance, often several retinal cells communicate with the brain via a single neural passageway—much like having several telephones on a party line. Such an arrangement is far less efficient than having a separate neural connection for each cell in the retina, and among hawks, owls, and most other birds, there is a significantly larger proportion of the "private line" connections. Moreover, hawks and other birds have a proportionately greater area of the brain devoted to vision than we do. All of these features combine to produce a visual sharpness that appears to be even more than eight times as great as human resolving power, as the following evidence suggests.

Recently a group of airborne observers learned something of a hawk's ability to see in the wild. The observers were using a glider plane to follow hawks migrating southward down the eastern U.S. mountain ranges. Hawks migrate almost effortlessly by soaring upward in a thermal, a column of warm, rising air that carries them aloft. From the great height at the top, the birds glide long distances to the base of another thermal, where they get another free lift upward. The observers in the glider plane found that hawks can see and home on other hawks in thermals as far as six miles away. To pose a human standard against this, Barry Kinzie and I recently tried to determine the distance limit at which we could detect hawks migrating along the Blue Ridge. We both have better than 20/20 vision, and we were using high-quality 8× and 9× binoculars. We found the practical limit at which we could detect hawks in normal atmospheric conditions to be between three and four miles as determined by USGS topographic maps. If a hawk could see "only" eight times as well as we do, they should have similar limits of vision; but apparently they see much better than the retinal-cell count alone suggests.

The extreme sharpness, or acuity, of a hawk's vision is augmented by its capacity to see color. A hawk's retina contains a high number of cone cells, and evidence from behavioral studies suggests that hawks make frequent use of color distinctions. However, though hawks are beautifully adapted to diurnal (daytime) activity, they see poorly in dim light. My own experience in falconry suggests that some hawks see less well in dim light than do humans.

All birds appear to see color to some degree and to see well in bright light, but some nocturnal (nighttime) birds have developed high proportions of rod cells throughout their retinas in order to see well in dim light. The best-known group of nocturnal birds is the owls, who have evolved fascinating adaptations for dim-light vision. Their eyes are shaped like tubes rather than spheres, and hence cannot be rotated in the sockets—owls have to turn their heads and look face-on at an object. But an owl's large, efficiently shaped eyes with large pupils and rod-rich retinas allow them to see in the dimmest light. They cannot see in total darkness, of course; but laboratory experiments with barn owls reveal that they can see well enough to "capture" a dummy mouse in light equivalent to that produced by a single match burning at a distance of 100 yards from the illuminated object. The experiments were carefully controlled to exclude all extraneous light, and also the owls' ears were closed with temporary plugs to prevent them from using sound as a homing device. The experimenters concluded that owls can see as well by starlight as we can see on an overcast day, and that a moonlit night is positively bright for an owl. Contrary to popular myth, however, owls are not blinded by daylight. I have seen great horned owls and barred owls hunting at high noon on cloudless days, and observed several other species of nocturnal owls functioning perfectly well in daylight. Some species (hawk owls, burrowing owls, snowy owls) are even diurnal; most simply prefer to be active at night because they hunt most efficiently in night conditions.

Owls (and, to a lesser extent, hawks) possess good binocular vision, with both eyes located well forward on the head so that they can be focused on an object simultaneously, presumably affording a three-dimensional image. All birds possess some frontal binocular vision, but most species differ from owls in having their eyes placed farther back and relatively high on the sides of their heads. Thus they have good monocular vision to either side and also a field of vision that extends much higher than that of an owl. Many such birds also have lens curvatures and flattened eyeballs that provide wide-field vision and enable them to scan large portions of the environment almost instantly. This is an evolutionary adaptation to enable them to escape the swift approach of a predator from the side, rear, or above. Many species can actually see 360 degrees without turning their heads—ducks are one example. One familiar species, the woodcock, has such extreme wide-angle vision that it has binocular vision not only forward of its head, but behind it as well! Most birds, even hawks, possess a greater degree of side vision than do humans.

These are some of the more interesting visual adaptations among a few species of birds. But there are about 645 species of native wild birds in North America north of Mexico. It should be obvious that not all birds can see in daylight as well as hawks, nor at night as well as owls, nor in such a wide angle as woodcocks. Nevertheless, out in the field it is safe for us to assume that any species of bird can resolve several times more detail than we, and, with the exception of owls, has a much wider field of vision than we. Ordinarily, long before a wild bird has been registered on our retinas, we have already been registered on its retinas, and in much greater detail.

The sense of vision among mammals

There are about 378 species of native wild mammals in North America north of Mexico. Most people never see but a small percentage of these species, because the great majority of wild mammals are nocturnal. Given this last fact, it is not surprising that most mammals are also colorblind. As far as I have been able to determine by searching through the literature on the subject, among mammals only the higher primates—man, apes, chimpanzees—and a limited number of rodents possess

This barred owl's highly specialized eyes enable it to see in the dimmest light. Concealed beneath its head feathers are large ear openings that enable it also to hear with extraordinary sensitivity.

Most mammals possess one or two senses much keener than the human equivalents, though mammals often differ markedly in their sensory development. Most cats, such as the common house cat (above) possess keen senses of sight and hearing and are well adapted for both day and night vision. Many dogs, such as the beagle (above, right), possess keen senses of smell and hearing, but poor eyesight.

cone cells and the ability to see color. This may seem a disadvantage until we recognize that eyes equipped only with rods are able to see almost equally well in a wide range of light conditions, from the brightest daylight to the darkest night. Most mammals—the primates being the most obvious exception—also have eyes placed somewhat to the sides of their heads, and therefore have, in addition to binocular vision to the front, some degree of monocular vision to either side. They thus have wider fields of vision than do humans.

Aside from these facts, very few generalizations can be made about the vision of mammals. A number of mammals unquestionably see better than we do, though it is doubtful that any mammal sees as well as hawks and owls. Among those that see well are the predators who depend upon vision while hunting, and prey species who escape capture by traveling at high speed over long distances. Typical of these types are some of the cats, wolves, antelopes, and deers. Among those who see poorly are species that are big and powerful enough to have few natural enemies, or that escape quickly by running short distances and diving into burrows or water. Typical of these types are moose, bears, woodchucks, and beavers. However, burrow- or den-living mammals that are small enough to be subject to the swift aerial attacks of hawks and owls usually have quite good vision, for obvious reasons.

One of the best ways to get an idea of the visual capacities of a mammalian species is to study a field guide or a life history. A written account is usually available in a local library. How much does the species depend on vision for food-gathering and survival? If it relies heavily on vision, you can be assured that the species possesses good vision; if it relies little on vision, then its eyesight may not be highly developed.

The sense of hearing among birds

Probably most birds hear better than humans. Certainly a few species have hearing capacities that are almost unimaginable. The reason may lie in the structure of the avian ear, which, compared to the mammalian ear, is a model of simplicity. Our own ear, from outside to inside, consists of an exterior lobe; a relatively long canal terminated by a membrane, the eardrum; three small bones connected in series and named for their shapes—hammer, anvil, and stirrup; and a shell-like inner organ called the cochlea, which is filled with fluid and lined with sensory cells. In a bird, the sequence is a short canal terminated by a drum; a single bone, the columella; and the inner ear. The more simple, direct system of a bird's ear probably enables it to hear sounds too faint to be registered at all by the human ear.

The same experimenters who investigated the visual capacities of barn owls also studied their ability to respond to sound in a laboratory under conditions of total darkness. They found that the owls needed only two very brief, very faint sound emissions from a radio speaker concealed beneath paper. The speaker was used to simulate the noises of a foraging mouse. At the first sound, the perched owls oriented themselves toward the speaker. At the second sound they launched into flight and plunged their talons through the paper with something like 80 percent accuracy to "capture" the simulated mouse. Humans placed near the owls' perches could not even hear the sounds from the speaker, much less pinpoint its location within an inch in three dimensions.

Probably most birds do not hear quite as well as barn owls, who prey heavily upon small nocturnal animals that forage for food beneath grass or fallen leaves. But in fact we really do not know how well most birds hear; it is difficult to design experiments to test the hearing of many species. But I can give two illustrations from personal observations. When I take my red-tailed hawk squirrel hunting, she frequently locates squirrels on the other sides of thickets by sounds which I cannot hear—and I have good hearing, by human standards. While perched on my fist she will stretch upward and move her head about in an attempt to see something; if she cannot see it, she will fly up onto a tree limb to gain a vantage point; and invariably this behavior pattern results in our finding a squirrel in the area in which she showed interest. This behavior is quite different from the pattern that follows a direct visual sighting. If while on the fist she sees a squirrel, she will either launch immediately into flight, or decide that the flight path is too thick for her to maneuver, and after a second or two will settle onto the fist in a rest position. The clear inference, then, is that her hearing is far superior to mine.

Another example. For years I have hunted and observed wild turkeys with my father, who has spent a lifetime studying these magnificent creatures. He has shown me convincingly that a turkey can pinpoint the location of a sound from several hundred yards through thick woods. Under certain circumstances, turkeys will come to an appropriate call. Time after time I have seen them come to the precise spot of a call which was issued only once. Sometimes they came by a direct route, sometimes by a circuitous, indirect route, but always without error. The birds had not merely to determine direction, they had also to judge distance; and both are made difficult by the sound of the call bouncing off trees and landforms, sometimes producing a misleading ventriloquistic effect to the human ear. Yet these birds can locate the sound accurately at one hearing, and their behavior indicates that they know the location of the sound to within a space of a few feet. These birds, which I believe can see almost as well as hawks, can apparently hear almost as well as owls.

I also know that many larger birds such as herons cannot be successfully approached by a person if he makes even a slight noise, even though he may be concealed from sight by landforms or other absolute obstructions to vision. It is difficult to judge the hearing capacities of many smaller birds—they permit close approach even when you are in full view, so it is difficult to know how sensitive their hearing is. But almost all species of birds use vocal calls to communicate various kinds of meanings, and studies show that these vocal signals often play key roles in such vital activities as food-finding, mating, and the rearing of young. Obviously, there is a great deal of selective pressure among wild birds to favor those with good hearing and eliminate those with poor hearing. In the field I always operate on the assumption that all birds hear better than I—and so far have no reason to regret that strategy.

One final word on bird hearing. During a recent visit to the Cornell Laboratory of Ornithology I learned from Dr. William Keeton that birds are adapted to hear infrasound—extremely low-pitched sound well below the human hearing range, detectable by us only with the aid of special equipment. Infrasound is especially interesting in that it can travel hundreds, even thousands of miles with very little loss of power. Using it, at least in theory, birds several hundred miles inland can listen to distant ocean surf, or to thunderstorms a thousand miles away, or to other things we do not yet know about. It seems likely to me that a human moving through the natural environment may sometimes produce infrasound noises, undetectable to himself, but obvious to a bird even a great distance away.

The wild turkey, a large ground-dwelling bird, possesses unusually keen senses of sight and hearing, making it one of the most difficult quarries for hunters and birders alike.

The sense of hearing among mammals

Most of us have had the experience, either directly or through the cinema, of seeing a wild deer react to a small sound. The deer jerks its head up and stands alert, nose testing the air for scent, eyes searching for a sign of movement, the big ears revolving turretlike as they search for a repetition of the sound. Many mammalian species possess large "directional" ears that can be turned within a limited range as an aid to hearing; all such species can be observed making constant use of their ears, and we should expect them to hear quite well. And in fact they do.

I received a good lesson in the acute hearing capacities of dogs when I was attending the Infantry Officers Course at Fort Benning, Georgia. One exercise was designed to acquaint us with the abilities of German shepherds from the Canine Corps to aid in the detection and apprehension of enemy infiltrators operating under darkness. My platoon was broken into small groups, the groups being placed at intervals of about a hundred yards along one of many dirt roads that crisscrossed the enormous wooded areas of the reservation. Each group was assigned a Canine Corps trainer and his dog. We would observe the dog's behavior as "enemy" infiltrators from the Infantry School staff attempted to move through our line undetected.

It was a bitter-cold February night. There were no cheerful insect sounds; the moon was a mere sliver in the iron sky; a fitful breeze blew from behind our left shoulders as we stood in the pale road peering into the dark woods ahead of us, or looking around at the dark woods behind us. Our breath shone silvery in the faint moonlight. Around our necks hung huge 10×50 "night glasses" issued especially for the occasion. We talked in low voices, stamping our feet to keep warm. After what seemed hours, the trainer spoke: "Okay—he's picked up an infiltrator. See if you can detect him." We looked in disbelief at the shepherd, who was merely sitting in the road beside his trainer, looking alertly into the woods to our front. "How can you tell he's got one?" somebody asked. "Because," the trainer said, "he's pointing. Watch the dog's nose." We did,

Many mammals, such as this deer, possess large "directional" ears that can be turned at will to enable the animal to hear with extreme sensitivity.

getting close and peering through the darkness. Sure enough, by a movement almost as imperceptible as that of the minute hand of a clock, the dog's nose was swinging ever so slowly to our right.

"The infiltrator's comin' up a road over there. See if you can hear him." We all turned and faced in the direction the dog was pointing. We stood still and listened. Some of us cupped hands behind the ears to hear better. We held our breath and stood statuelike, straining every nerve to hear something, anything that sounded like a human on the move. The only sound was the faint stirring of the breeze through the pines. Finally came expressions of disbelief; the dog was wrong, there was no one out there, the people who were supposed to be running the exercise were probably asleep somewhere in a nice warm building, the whole exercise was worthless anyway. The trainer remained calm. Still the dog's muzzle swung to the right. We tried to look into the woods with our binoculars. It was hopeless. The woods were an impenetrable tangle of second-growth trees. We listened some more. Utter silence, save for the wind.

"Okay," the trainer said. "He's just about ready to step into the road up to our right. Put your glasses up and you should be able to see him step out." We raised the big glasses and focused them on an intersection about seventy yards up—it was plainly visible through the big optics. "He should be coming out . . ." said the trainer, pausing for dramatic effect, "just about *now*." And almost instantly a man appeared in the road. We glanced at the dog, whose muzzle pointed directly toward the "enemy." We considered that the breeze had ruled out the possibility of the dog's tracking the infiltrator by scent and also had made hearing more difficult. It was a convincing demonstration, for none of us ever heard any sounds; yet the dog tracked them for a good twenty minutes as the man approached us from a considerable distance. All up and down our road that night, other shepherds had performed similar feats. Impressive.

I suspect that many species of wild mammals hear just as well as those shepherds, which had not been selectively bred for hearing ability, but rather for intelligence and trainability. On the other hand, there are probably some species of mammals that hear only about as well as we do. I suspect that many wild mammals, regardless of species, lose some hearing ability in old age just as humans do, though I have no convincing proof of this. But certainly all wild mammals appear to be much more alert to and aware of the sounds around them than we are, and thus make better use of the equipment they have.

The sense of smell among birds

Recent research suggests that most birds possess a sense of smell, but as far as is presently known, very few rely upon it in significant ways. Their way of life predisposes them to rely heavily upon vision and hearing. Examination of the portion of the brain that responds to smells (the olfactory lobes) shows this area to be very poorly developed in birds as compared to mammals. This is not surprising, since many birds spend a great deal of time in flight or on perches high above the ground. Since most stimuli to the sense of smell are heavy gases that tend to remain low in the atmosphere, birds in flight or on high perches have little opportunity to rely on smell as a significant way of sensing the environment. Even when they fly low to the ground, the speed of their flight would create great difficulty for them in sniffing out subtle odors. Perhaps significantly, the species of birds which may make use of smell in locating food are all ground dwellers. The kiwi, a flightless nocturnal bird of New Zealand, feeds on worms, which it apparently locates by smell. Some people believe that ducks and woodcocks make use of their sense of smell, and I know a few hunters who believe that the wild turkey does, though these claims are uncertain. On the other hand, some species behave as if they have no sense of smell, or perhaps very strange preferences among odors. The great horned owl, for instance, seems to consider fresh skunk the greatest of delicacies; and in capturing one of these creatures the owl is often sprayed so thoroughly that its plumage retains the odor for months, or until the bird molts in new plumage. Some museum specimens of great horned owls have retained the odor for years. The skunk's powerful scent, however, has no deterrent effect upon the owl, who seems not the least bothered by it.

Among North American species the only bird that is known to base significant behavior upon smell is the turkey vulture. Closely related to the hawks (though some claim it is more closely related to storks), this timid bird is our continent's unrivaled master of thermals and air currents. With its enormous wings outspread, it rides the air for hours on end with never a wingbeat, soaring in great circles over its territory, sustained in flight entirely by sun- and wind-generated energy. At heights ranging from just above the treetops to thousands of feet, it searches for carrion. It uses both its keen eyesight (comparable to a hawk's) and its sense of smell to locate food as it soars slowly over its hunting ground. However, its close relative and lookalike, the black vulture, appears to rely upon sight alone, and often upon the sight of a turkey vulture landing or feeding on food it has located. The black vulture, being more aggressive, will then drive off the turkey vulture and steal its food. An interesting study of the part of the brain concerned with smell in these two species has shown that the olfactory lobes of the turkey vulture are three times larger than those of the black vulture. In short, though a few species of birds appear to have a useful sense of smell, most do not; and as observers in the wild, we can virtually ignore the possibility of birds detecting us with this sense.

The sense of smell among mammals

If an insignificant number of bird species appear to base behavior on a sense of smell, the situation is reversed among mammals: only an insignificant number of species appear *not* to have the sense well developed. And we humans count heavily among the insignificant numbers. We have, of course, a sense of smell, but compared to that of most other mammalian species, ours is almost nonexistent, at best rudimentary, virtually useless in the wild when it comes to detecting the presence of creatures except those with extremely rank odors.

All living creatures have odors, because they constantly exude an invisible "spray" of molecules that pass out of the body through the mouth and nose, and the pores and glands on the body surface. Some of these molecules are heavier than air and quickly settle downward, leaving a trail where we have passed. Others are relatively buoyant in air and may float about for some time, often traveling considerable distances in air currents. Either way, when these molecules strike a sufficiently sensitive olfactory organ, they trigger a complex chemical reaction and are registered as "odors." Apparently each species of bird and mammal produces a distinctive species odor, for dogs and other mammals readily distinguish between the scent trails of different species, whether prey or enemy. Moreover, each member of a species seems to have its own peculiar individual odor, for mammals readily recognize individuals (mates, members of family or social units, familiar acquaintances or enemies) by scent alone. To us humans, it is a complex, bewildering world, this world of scents.

And in truth it is a subtle world. Even humans can detect some odors if as little as one thirty-billionth part by weight is present in a volume of air. A human's olfactory tissue, located in the upper part of the nasal passages, is not very large and is relatively smooth. In most other mammals, however, the olfactory tissue is proportionately much larger and is intricately folded, ridged, and convoluted to expose more surface (and sensory cells) to incoming air. The resulting increase in surface area can be astonishing. In a cottontail rabbit, for instance, the olfactory surface is eight times as great as the exterior surface area of the body. Most mammal species are equipped with much larger and more sensitive olfactory surfaces than we, and as a result can detect odor-producing molecules that form such an infinitesimal percentage of air volume that it is pointless for us even to talk about the figures. We all know about the remarkable sense of smell in dogs. Not only dogs, of course, but *most* mammalian species are capable of following a scent trail left by another creature hours, even days, before; of detecting the presence of another animal up to a mile away if the wind is right; of routinely detecting the presence of food, friends, and enemies that could not be detected by either vision or hearing. If carried some distance away from their territories, they can even find the way home by using environmental odors as a guide.

The sense of smell is extremely valuable to most wild mammals, and they rely heavily upon it in most of their significant behavior. It is impossible for us to imagine a world in which things are perceived in terms of scent impressions that are just as vivid as our own sight impressions, perhaps even more vivid. Yet for most mammalian species, this is how the world is perceived. When dealing with wild mammals, we must constantly keep in mind that a rich world of odors, as invisible and unknowable to us as another dimension of space or time, exists all around us and that we are a significant fact in that world. Only with this knowledge in mind can we begin to understand that our presence, no matter how silent or how well concealed from view, may still trigger powerful reactions in most mammals.

II

HOW WILD ANIMALS AVOID DETECTION AND DANGER

So any healthy animal we are likely to encounter in the wild has at least one and possibly two or three senses much better than ours. Combine this with the animal's constant alertness to its environment and it becomes obvious that being close to a wild bird or mammal and remaining undetected—or at least appearing harmless—requires something other than our ordinary behavior. If you and I walked through woods and fields as if hurrying to the post office the creatures around us would regard us as dangerous and take evasive action—the environment would seem almost completely devoid of birds and mammals. Yet thirty minutes after we had passed through, a good observer could enter the same area and see it teeming with wildlife. What became of all the creatures while we were hurrying through? And what did another person do differently that enabled him to see all sorts of wildlife where we could see none? Let's answer these questions in turn.

In normal circumstances, when wild creatures feel threatened by an enemy they will seek to do one of three things: to avoid detection; to flee; or, rarely, to attack. (While they have young in a nest or den, many species will undertake a fourth response, a "broken-wing" or "crippled" act that serves to lure the enemy from the vicinity of the young.) Basically, these three goals are accomplished by one or more of the following methods.

Concealment. Most wild creatures are surprisingly adept at concealing themselves behind screens of leaves, tree trunks, bushes, grass, fallen logs, rocks, mounds of earth, roadbanks, and just about anything else available. When frightened, a squirrel will hide behind a tree trunk or limb; a bird will go behind thick foliage; a deer will stand behind bushes; a mouse will hide beneath a leaf or log. Some animals appear especially to seek to hide their eyes from an observer, since a bright eye often attracts attention to itself.

Freezing. Frequently when a wild creature seeks to escape notice it will freeze, or remain motionless. This not only makes the animal less obvious to vision, but also to hearing and, to some extent, to smell, since movement increases the number of scent molecules emitted from the body. Freezing is often combined with concealment. Freezing is more effective against wild animals than against man, as will be explained later.

Cryptic coloration. Some animals do not need to conceal themselves behind anything, because they are so colored, shaped, and marked that their outlines seem to break up and blend almost perfectly into their natural surroundings; they need only freeze to become all but invisible. A gray squirrel is the color of tree bark; a grouse the color of the forest floor; a meadowlark the color of dry grass. A bittern stretches itself upward and its shape and color cause it to disappear into the surrounding marsh grasses; an owl is shaped so as to appear to have no neck or head, and, motionless high up in a tree, blends into the color of the bark and appears to be merely a piece of broken limb. Of course, many animals do not possess cryptic coloration; but some have such effective coloration as to be invisible even when their location is known. I have seen newly hatched wild quail disappear before my eyes at a freeze command from their mother, and I could find them in the fallen leaves only by moving a small twig gently over the surface of the ground until it touched one of the chicks, whereupon it would scurry a few inches away and disappear again.

Stealthy escape. Many times a wild creature will attempt to escape from his enemy by stealth, attempting, as it were, both to avoid detection and to put distance between itself and the enemy. The animal will move quietly away, usually crouched down and almost always attempting to conceal itself behind some obstacle to vision. I have watched from a distant vantage point as a deer used this technique to escape the detection of friends of mine who were fairly close to it. I've watched a male turkey step behind a tree and vanish completely, apparently moving quietly away while keeping the tree between it and me with cunning accuracy. Turkeys will sometimes escape by leaping from a high bluff or ridge and sailing downhill, thus avoiding the necessity of flapping their large, noisy wings. Many swimming birds are quite good at stealthy escape, and will swim to safety either above or below water (depending on the species) with nary a telltale sound.

Rapid escape. Sometimes an animal will not care whether it is detected in escape or not; it just moves away as rapidly as it can, frequently with a great deal of noise as well as speed. A deer may take leaps of thirty feet and attain speeds faster than a racehorse; a duck may leap from the water and speed away at over fifty miles per hour. Many times the fleeing animal will soon disappear behind trees or landforms, utilizing the principle of concealment to augment its escape.

Social warning systems. An observer should be aware that if he frightens one animal of field or forest, that animal is likely to sound the alarm to all other animals in the immediate area. A frightened beaver slaps its tail on the water and all the beavers around the pond dive for protection. If there are ducks on the pond, they will probably scurry into cover or immediately take flight, squawking the alarm. Most small birds and mammals near the pond will seek concealment, freeze, and virtually disappear. A scene formerly busy with the activities of wild creatures is now silent and motionless save for some spreading ripples on the pond's surface.

Another instance. I have flown my hawk at squirrels foraging on the floor of a deciduous woods with a very dense squirrel population. The eastern gray squirrel (*Sciurus carolinensis*) has a peculiar alarm call, a kind of gibberish, which I have heard only when the squirrel is frightened by a flying hawk. When my hawk took wing, the first squirrel to notice her would break immediately into a wild dash and at the same time begin emitting gibberish, and as if by magic every squirrel within sight and earshot was also immediately dashing for a tree and spouting gibberish. This social warning system, apparent in many species, has two major functions: it protects all members of the species in the immediate area by sounding the alarm; and it protects the one who sounded the alarm by creating a melee of escape activity that may distract or confuse the enemy. It also warns other species of the danger in the area. Ingenious; and it works, too.

Special defenses. For the sake of thoroughness, a few special animal defenses should be mentioned. These are unusual means of defense not possessed by most species of animals and not belonging to any of the above categories. Some examples: the armadillo's armored plates, which form a protective shield when it rolls itself into a ball; the skunk's scent glands, which emit a powerful, repellent odor; and the porcupine's quills, barbed needles which inflict intense pain. Animals that possess these kinds of defenses are normally unaggressive and will not attack a human unless provoked.

Attack. Any bird or mammal will attack an enemy as a last resort: a cornered rabbit will turn upon a fox, a sparrow flown to the ground by a hawk will turn on its pursuer. Since the animal that turns in these circumstances is desperate, though it may be relatively harmless it tries to appear as ferocious as possible. It puffs out its fur or feathers, assumes threatening postures, and hisses, growls, shrieks, or makes some other threatening noise, depending on its species. Sometimes the ruse works and the more powerful attacker pauses long enough for its victim to escape. Most creatures will turn upon a human in circumstances where they feel trapped or threatened, but even though the animal may be relatively harmless, a thoughtful person does not put animals in terrifying situations any more than he would put members of his family in such situations.

We should note that some animals, by virtue of their size or natural weapons, should be considered extremely dangerous if they or their young are placed in threatening circumstances. While no North American bird could be considered "deadly" to man, many of the larger hawks and owls can inflict deep cuts with their talons. The greatest danger from these birds is probably damage to the eyes, for many hawks and owls seem to have an instinctive knowledge of the vulnerability of these organs to their talons. Among mammals, most of the larger species can be dangerous. A female moose, for instance, who finds a human between her and her young can put 1,500 pounds of bone, hard muscle, and flying hooves into an incredibly rapid charge. Almost any large predator—a grizzly, a puma, a timber wolf—can be a deadly adversary because of its size, strength, and natural weapons. However, the big predators seldom turn on humans unless they are cornered or wounded, their young are threatened, or they are driven by extreme hunger. Most of the big predators now exist only in remnant populations and must struggle to maintain themselves in ever-shrinking areas of suitable habitat. These magnificent creatures have been victimized for centuries by the senseless persecution of the misinformed. Thankfully, they are now protected by legislation and are being carefully managed to ensure their survival. If you should come upon one of these creatures in the wild, treat it with awe and respect. It may be vastly superior to you in courage and strength; but by virtue of your superior brain you can recognize and appreciate what it can never comprehend—that it is one of a vanishing species and that it needs your compassion if its kind is to be saved from the utter finality of extinction. Regard the creature with wonder, and leave it alone.

Why do animals fear man? In North America, with the exception of animals caring for young, only the larger bears and a few rutting ungulates will ordinarily advance upon a human. Even the puma and wolf, powerful and well armed as they are, will go to great lengths to avoid detection by or contact with man. Why?

It is too easy and facile to answer that man is the greatest predator of all, having killed so many members of some species that only those with a genetically encoded fear of man survived. That is both more and less than the truth. Certainly, birds in the Galápagos Islands display what appears to be an extremely diminished fear of man, allowing themselves to be approached quite closely. One could assume that these birds have little fear of man because they have no previous experience with him, since the islands have been uninhabited by humans until recent years. But the picture may be larger than this. For most of the birds of the Galápagos there are no predators of any kind, and the birds consequently have a diminished fear of all other species; the fact that they do not fear man is merely incidental. In North America the situation is almost unimaginably different, for predation is a way of life for almost every species, and the individual who does not learn to be wary may quickly end up being someone else's meal. Thus most species of wild animals in North America have learned to keep a safe distance between themselves and other species that they do not specifically recognize as harmless, and ordinarily, of course, this includes man. But in fact animals have quite complex spatial requirements that determine how they relate to their immediate family and other members of their species as well as to members of different species, and looking at those requirements will help us understand a good deal of animal behavior.

Each animal has a zone or "bubble" of private space that it carries with it wherever it goes. This bubble disappears for members of the individual's family or social group, but may take varying sizes for strangers. We humans exhibit the same behavior. We easily admit into our private bubble members of our own family and feel comfortable being close to them and touching them. But we do not like strangers to invade this bubble, to come closer than what we feel is a "correct" distance for talking to strangers. If a stranger does stand too close during a conversation, we tend to experience feelings of uneasiness and hostility—we have the impulse either to back away or to shove the intruder back to the "correct" distance. Curiously, the size of our private space bubble is determined by our cultures. People from northern European cultures, for example, tend to stand relatively far apart when talking with strangers, people from southern European cultures much closer. Thus when Mr. Windsor, an Anglo-American, confronts Mr. Vitello, an Italian-American, Mr. Windsor feels that Mr. Vitello is standing too close, and backs away to his idea of the "correct" conversational distance; Mr. Vitello, feeling that he is now too far away, advances closer to his idea of the "correct" distance, and again Mr. Windsor feels he must back away. The sizes of their bubbles differ because of their different cultural backgrounds. When they part, without quite knowing why, perhaps, Mr. Windsor will consider Mr. Vitello "pushy"; and Mr. Vitello will consider Mr. Windsor "standoffish." Quite so.

Now, we have to use our imaginations a bit to understand that in addition to our private-space bubbles, we also have much larger "safety zones" around us which emerge when we confront other, dangerous species in the wild. This area or zone expands or contracts, depending upon circumstances. If we were backpacking in the Rockies and saw a grizzly bear two miles away on the next mountainside, we would feel no fear. But if the animal approached closer and closer, ultimately an invisible border would be crossed and the animal would intrude upon our safety zone for grizzlies; we would feel alarm and probably take protective action. If the intruder were a porcupine, the zone might not be as large, but it would still exist.

Both the private-space bubble and the safety-zone concepts can be applied to wild animals. Almost all animals display a private-space bubble in relation to unfamiliar members of their own, closely related, or competing species. The bubble sometimes expands to become a large territory with fixed geographical limits; at other times it shrinks and becomes almost nonexistent, and individuals that once fought over territory then fraternize gregariously. Most North American animals also display safety zones in relation to members of dangerous species. Exactly how an animal recognizes a dangerous species is uncertain, but there are three possibilities. In the first case, the individual animal may have learned fear of another species as a result of a hostile encounter, or by direct experience. A cat who has been chased by a dog, for example, becomes wary of all dogs. In the second case, the individual animal, while young, may have learned fear of another species by observing and imitating the behavior of its parents, or by indirect experience. Young crows, for example, soon learn from their parents to stay well away from a human carrying a gun, even though the young themselves have no prior direct experience with hunters. In the third case, the individual animal may have an innate, genetically encoded fear of another species. Young birds reared in complete isolation, for example, are terrified by the sight of a soaring falcon even though they could not possibly have had either direct or indirect experience with falcons. We should also bear in mind that many small animals probably regard very large animals as dangerous not so much because of their species as their size—quite sensibly, they are uncomfortable in close proximity to another creature whose bulk may be hundreds of times greater than their own. In any case, by whatever means wild animals acquire a fear of man, most display rather large safety zones where we are concerned and are easily aroused to protective action by our presence. In general, the larger the animal, the larger its safety zone. Small creatures like chickadees and chipmunks will permit relatively close approach before displaying an alarm reaction; larger creatures like turkeys and deer have much larger safety zones and will take alarm at much greater distances.

Undoubtedly a number of factors determine how a wild animal perceives and handles its spatial requirements, but as for the question of what triggers alarm reactions to humans, two things stand out in my experience. These are the individual animal's psychophysiological condition, and its interpretation of a human's intentions. Since both are very difficult to determine, I can only offer something in the way of speculation about how these things operate in the wild.

You and I know what it is like to be extremely hungry or emotionally upset—we tend to become irritable and snappish, to feel mean and just a little bit prone to violence. The same is true among animals—you can surely think of illustrations from your household dog or cat. But these domesticated creatures lead easy, secure lives compared to wild animals, most of which must hunt their food from day to day and live under constant threat of attack by a predator. Let me cite one example of how conditions of hunger affect an animal's psychological state. Falconers who keep hawks year-round fatten the birds during the summer molting season, feeding them literally all the food they can eat. The purpose is to speed the molting process and ensure strong feathers by providing an abundance of protein. A fat hawk is actually a lazy, docile creature. It likes nothing better than to bathe and sun itself early in the morning, then sit on its perch all day, standing first on one foot, then the other, watching the world go by. Later, when the molt is complete, the falconer reduces the bird's rations and over a period of about two weeks reduces its weight by 10 percent. The change in the size of the bird is barely apparent; but the change in its psychological state is striking and sometimes surprising.

The once relaxed bird that merely looked at you keenly now glares into your eyes with a fierce intensity; rather than standing docilely with one foot drawn up into its tail feathers, it stands alert on both feet; it shows an inclination to fly at small animals, becomes obstreperous and difficult to handle, and in a fit of irritation may sink its talons into the falconer himself. The hawk is in a state called *yarak*, an Arabic word with no English equivalent. It means that the bird is in hunting condition; psychologically, it is set to kill. It is by no means starved—it could easily withstand an additional 20 percent drop in its weight—but its emotions are obviously highly volatile and it is constantly on the verge of an angry rage.

Now we should not expect all hungry animals to exhibit a psychological state equivalent to *yarak*. But probably most wild creatures in a state of hunger (or pain) are more irritable, nervous, and skittish than when well fed and comfortable, and are likely to spook more quickly at the sight of a human than they would otherwise. Contrariwise, an animal that is hungry enough will also risk close proximity to man if such a risk involves food. You can observe both responses at a bird feeder during a heavy snow. Birds will come to the feeder even though you are standing close by; but they are very nervous and become violently alarmed at the slightest provocation. Also, an animal remains upset for a time after a harrowing experience with an enemy or a hostile encounter with a member of its own species. In this condition, too, the animal is nervous and testy. In short, an animal that is psychologically or physiologically irritated will probably have a much larger safety zone where man is concerned than will a fat, content animal.

Another factor determining the size of an animal's safety zone is its interpretation of a human's intentions. Animals seem to interpret a person's activities as either "harmless" or "threatening," often with uncanny accuracy. I have heard this attributed to a sixth sense, but my own opinion, formed largely from reading ethological studies, is that animals are able to read our body language, the postures and movements with which we unknowingly convey our intentions. We can use body language knowingly. If in approaching a wild animal I use an upright posture with my hands in my pockets, it will allow me to approach more closely than if I crouch slightly and carry my hands at about chest height as if ready to snatch or grasp at something. This is an obvious example, however, and I'm sure that animals are capable of reading much more subtle signals, signals that we are not even aware of.

Two forms of human behavior especially seem to discomfit many wild animals. One is for a human to stand over or appear to tower over them. In nature, one animal stands over another when it wishes to victimize or dominate it. The predator usually holds down its victim to inflict death; when members of the same species compete for dominance, the stronger usually ends up standing over the weaker. For example, when two dogs meet and test each other's strength, the confrontation frequently ends with the dominant dog standing over the weaker, which may lie on its back and expose the soft under-side of its body in a gesture of submission. Most ground-living birds and mammals have nowhere near the height of humans, and perceive us, even at some distance, as towering over them in a dominant, intimidating position. These creatures have no inclination to make gestures of submission to a strange species; they would much rather seek the safety of distance, and consequently flee or take other protective actions. An aware observer will, in the wild, be aware of this innate response in animals and may devise ways to minimize it.

Another discomfiting gesture to many animals is a direct, head-on stare, especially if prolonged. In the wild, the precursor to a predator's attack is almost always a direct stare in which the killer gauges the victim's distance, possible escape routes, and state of alertness. Some wild animals will bolt almost immediately in response to a direct stare. In the early stages of training a newly trapped hawk, falconers avoid looking directly into the bird's eyes, for such a gesture will frequently trigger a flurry of wing-flapping and jumping in an attempt to es-cape. Even a well-trained hawk can be made nervous by a stare from an unfamiliar person. Not all species are affected by a head-on gaze—many small birds, especially, seem oblivious to the human gaze. But most larger birds and most mammals, in my experience, show signs of uneasiness if a nearby human observer turns a head-on gaze toward them for a prolonged time. Averting the face to one side helps allay the animal's fear; so does the use of binoculars, which conceal the eyes and apparently, to the animal, do not resemble eyes.

What animals fear most. With exceptions so few that they can be counted on the fingers, every wild bird and mammal in North America lives under the constant threat of attack at any moment by a natural enemy. Every one of these animals must be always watchful for two things: a creature as large or larger than itself; and rapid movement, the swift rush that characterizes an attack. Swift movement in particular is important, for often it is the only thing a victim has time to see before the lightninglike strike of the predator. The creature who pauses to take a second look is doomed, and over the millennia the pressures of natural selection have been enormous toward producing instant responses to quick movement in the nearby environment. It is therefore an axiom that the one thing guaranteed to trigger escape, evasion, or defense reactions in our wild animals is a swift, rapid movement, particularly when it is made within the animal's safety zone by something as large as a human, and emphatically if it is made in the direction of the animal itself. Flight almost inevitably results; a skunk will turn tail, and a puma just might come down on your head, but most creatures will make a dash for safety.

One of the most important ingredients in successful wildlife observation, then, is either to conceal movement or to keep it minimal, slow, and deliberate. In fact, if a person could eliminate movement altogether he would become virtually invisible to wild animals. This seems incredible, especially in light of the superior vision of all birds and many mammals; nevertheless, it is true. This is why animals freeze as a protective measure; they become invisible even to the hawk or owl, those creatures whose vision is so far superior to ours. I am not saying here that when a person or animal freezes he disappears from view; rather, he is invisible in the sense that in the eyes of a wild animal he is no longer recognizable for what he is. The principle was vividly illustrated for me the first time I chanced upon a wild rabbit in the open after I had acquired and trained a hawk. With the bird on my fist I rounded the corner of a farm building and stopped abruptly when I saw a cottontail in some clover about twenty feet away. I fully expected the hawk to spring into flight, for the rabbit was in full view; but incredibly the hawk appeared not to see it at all. I soon realized that because it was motionless she saw it as just a form, a part of the landscape. I slowly squatted down and picked up a small pebble, which I tossed into the weeds behind the rabbit. When the pebble struck, one of the rabbit's ears revolved in that direction and within a heartbeat the hawk was in flight, and a split second later the rabbit was running for all it was worth.

Animals, it appears, have a different psychology of perception than you and I. Whereas we can visually recognize animal forms even when they are motionless, most wild creatures seem unable to recognize the same forms unless they are in motion. This is a vast and important difference, and an aspiring observer would do well to ponder its significance. That animals do not recognize a human who is motionless is common knowledge to every competent outdoorsman, but I would like to quote one whom I especially admire. He is Eliot Porter, whose incomparable wildlife photographs are evidence of a mastery of animal psychology and behavior. In his book *Birds of North America: A Personal Selection* (New York: E. P. Dutton, 1972), Porter says

The secret of wildlife observation is obvious enough—and, in truth, no secret at all—for it merely requires close attentiveness to all the minutiae of what goes on around one, made possible by a stillness of posture so that to other creatures one becomes just another object in nature. On numerous occasions I have found myself treated like an inanimate feature of the environment until I moved, when [the nearby animal] . . . suddenly took fright.

Some of my most memorable observations of wildlife have been made during periods of sitting motionless in woodlands. I have found that even though I remain as motionless as I can, it is rare that an animal approaches very close without finally noticing my presence. Mammals will usually pick up the scent of a human at close range, and birds are keen-eyed enough to see the slight movements that accompany breathing and focusing and blinking the eyes. I have come to expect one of three kinds of reactions when animals do finally detect my presence. One reaction is unqualified alarm—the animal will leap with surprise, then wheel and race off at the greatest possible speed until it disappears in the distance. At the opposite end of the spectrum is aroused curiosity—a mammal will stand and stretch its neck forward, sniffing the air and looking and listening with obvious curiosity; a bird will move around and cock its head from side to side to get a better view and perhaps utter scold notes or tentative alarm notes. Often the bird or mammal will approach, ever so cautiously, inch by inch, occasionally jumping back nervously, and then inching forward again to investigate further. During such an episode I find it extremely difficult to remain still because to me such behavior from an animal is downright funny and powerful stimulus to laughter.

This "curiosity" response usually ends in the third kind of reaction animals may display when they realize they have stumbled into close company with a human—a kind of combination of the two responses already described. The animal flees to what it considers a safe distance and then stops to look back, displaying curiosity over the nature of the intruder. Sometimes following this reaction the animal will return for a closer look; sometimes it will decide to flee even farther; and sometimes it will settle down to wait for the observer to reveal his intentions by moving. I have never been able to wait out an animal who chose this course. Animals, with no concept of time corresponding to our own, have enormous patience in such circumstances.

Rarely, when an animal exhibits curiosity over an observer's presence, the observer may make very slow movements without frightening the creature. I have sometimes been able to raise binoculars or a camera and aim them at a nearby deer or grouse; and both, while alert and ready to charge away, were nevertheless curious enough about the movements to stand their ground and watch. The movements must, however, be agonizingly slow. And with a camera in these circumstances I have never been able to shoot more than one frame because the click of the shutter always resulted in the animal's fleeing.

In short, when a human enters a natural area walking rapidly and noisily along, it is easy to predict what will happen: most wild creatures will disappear. However, when a human enters the same area to observe wild animals in proper fashion as will shortly be described, it is almost impossible to predict what will happen. The possibility of the unexpected—and the element of suspense—is always present. Of course one could generalize about a given species and say that normally it will permit approach to within such-and-such a distance; it is possible in a general way to compare and contrast the behavior of different species. But such abstractions are practically worthless in the field. It is virtually impossible to anticipate the behavioral differences shown by individual members of a given species. Some will be unusually wild, some will be unusually tame; a great deal depends on the individual animal's genetic endowment, previous experience, and psychophysiological condition. There are also quirks of landscape, vegetation, and weather conditions that may make an observer less noticeable to an animal situated in a certain spot and make possible an unusually close approach. Again, one may come upon an animal so preoccupied that it fails to notice the observer's presence or is undisturbed by it.

This last principle was illustrated recently when I approached a group of mobbing crows by walking stealthily through a thick stand of pines. When I emerged at the edge of the pines, not thirty yards away in the hardwoods beyond was a great horned owl, regal and magnificent in the morning sunlight, glaring at the crows, which stood on nearby branches cawing loudly. The owl was clutching a partly eaten opossum in one foot, and occasionally lunged at one of the crows, clacking its beak, to scare off its tormentors. I noticed that one of the crows seemed unusually large, and when I saw its wedge-shaped tail I recognized it as a raven. This was almost as astonishing as finding the owl clutching an opossum in the trees, for ravens seldom venture into the central part of Virginia, where this scene was taking place. It soon became apparent that the raven was much bolder toward the owl than were the crows. It would approach quite close to the owl, and when the owl clacked its beak the raven would lean forward and imitate the sound. In human terms, it seemed to be mocking and taunting the owl. About this time the crows noticed my presence and, giving alarm calls, flew off in a group. The raven lingered, perhaps tempted by the meal the owl was clutching; then it too noticed me, flew swiftly in a circle over my head, croaked, and flew away after the crows. The owl continued to perch in the tree, occasionally looking down at me as I watched it through binoculars, but seemingly less concerned with my presence than with the possibility of the crows returning, for it continued looking about in all directions, stopping only now and then to snatch a bite of its meal. In the sunlight it was incredibly beautiful, every feather perfect, its eyes the purest imaginable yellow. There was nothing dreamy about them, however; they glared fiercely, betokening the power and terrible ferocity of the creature that has aptly been nicknamed "the tiger of the air"—a creature that knows almost no fear in nature, but is extremely shy of man and one of the most difficult to observe in daytime. After watching it for perhaps five minutes, I slowly backed into the pines, so as not to frighten it, and walked away. It is the constant possibility of the unusual, the unexpected, and the unpredictable event such as this which makes wildlife observation so keenly pleasurable.

We have reviewed some of the more important responses wild animals display toward human intruders into their world. Now it is time to discuss some of the basic techniques of entering their world with the least possible disturbance.

III

TECHNIQUES: STALKING AND STILL- HUNTING

The two most basic ways of seeing animals are by stalking and by still-hunting. Both of these terms have developed a variety of meanings. I use *stalking* in the original sense of "to move by stealth," and *still-hunting* in the sense of "to remain motionless with the expectation that quarry will approach." In a sense, stalking is the observer going to the animals; still-hunting is the observer letting the animals come to him. Both techniques are basic because neither requires the use of lures, calls, or other inducements to control animal behavior; and neither requires the use of blinds. However, both techniques, as will be seen, are adaptable to a variety of employments ranging from the simple and easy to the complex and difficult.

STALKING

Stalking is indisputably fun. The only required equipment is a pair of binoculars. Beyond that, the beginner may want a field guide to aid in identification. The more experienced may or may not want to carry any of the following: telescope; gun or bow; gunstock camera or movie camera; sound-recording equipment; notebook; sketchpad; or anything else suited to his interests and needs. In stalking, the novice will find excitement in discovering and correctly identifying common species. The intermediate stalker will know the pleasure of seeing common species as old friends and of finding the uncommon species that require more rigorous searching. The advanced stalker will know nerve-tingling tension as he attempts to locate and approach the really rare and difficult species that are seen in their natural state by only a tiny percentage of the human population. Stalking can be physically easy, suitable even for patients with heart problems or other disabilities for which mild exercises are prescribed. (There are even some excellent wheelchair stalkers who utilize special park trails.) On the other hand, stalking can be strenuous enough to require the physical fitness of a professional athlete. It can, in short, be just about anything the individual wants to make of it. For convenience of discussion, I have more or less arbitrarily chosen three points along the range of difficulty that can be encountered in stalking. There are, of course, gradients of difficulty between these three points with requirements and advantages that can be readily grasped after even a few brief experiences in the field.

Basic stalking

Most common goals: Viewing small land and shore birds and the less-shy small mammals at close range, and waterfowl and larger birds and mammals at longer range.

Typical walking: Along residential streets, park trails, back roads, woods roads, field edges, beaches—wherever suitable habitat is found and walking is easy.

Physical demands: Mild to moderate, depending on terrain, weather conditions, and time spent in the field.

Special clothing required: None. Clothing need only be comfortable and appropriate for terrain and weather conditions; good footwear should be a strong consideration.

Equipment needed: Binoculars. For long-range viewing, a telescope mounted on a gunstock or tripod. Other equipment as desired.

Cautions: In hunting season in areas open to hunting, blaze-orange clothing is strongly recommended.

In basic stalking you do not rely on personal concealment; rather, you subdue your movements and sounds in order to appear harmless and rely on the small safety zones of some animals to allow you to make a close approach. Small birds, because of their powers of rapid flight and escape, have much smaller safety zones than common small diurnal mammals. Most small birds and mammals, however, will allow a harmless-appearing human to approach close enough for excellent viewing through general-purpose binoculars. Many small birds, in fact, will tolerate distances of only a few feet, too close for the focusing range of many binoculars. Brightly colored clothing is of little or no consequence if you are interested primarily in the small species that allow close approach. It may be a disadvantage, however, if you hope to see the larger, shyer species that may be in the area but will flee from a human presence as soon as it is detected within the animal's very large safety zone. Clothing of subdued colors helps minimize early detection.

The stalking technique is to walk slowly and quietly along, pausing frequently to look and listen for evidence of wildlife. (If you are interested in seeing mammals, you should walk into the wind to prevent your scent from being carried forward and frightening them well before they're in viewing range.) As soon as a quarry is spotted, you can slowly raise your binoculars for a better look. At this time it is extremely important to avoid making loud noises or sudden, rapid movements. If you want a closer look you can move slowly and cautiously toward the animal; but as soon as you cross the boundary of its safety zone it will flee. A good rule of thumb is to get only as close as you need for your purposes, then stop at a good vantage point and study the animal at leisure. It helps if you seat yourself; this not only puts the animal at ease, but also enables you to rest your elbows on your knees and look comfortably through your binoculars for an extended time.

Birders will undoubtedly want to employ calling techniques to bring small field and woods birds into better viewing circumstances. For reliable techniques, read the appropriate section in the chapter "Getting Birds and Mammals to Come to You." It is also possible, though less reliable, to call various mammals during such outings.

If one of the very shy species is spotted—say a hawk or a deer—you should freeze until the animal's attentions are directed elsewhere, then quietly take advantage of whatever measures you can to make yourself less visible. If you succeed you can then view your quarry as long as circumstances permit. For some important points on reducing your visibility in these situations, read the next section on intermediate stalking.

There are a number of pleasures associated with basic stalking. One is seeing a variety of birds and mammals and almost always having something unexpected or unusual occur. Another pleasure derives from the possibilities of human companionship. Since concealment is only rarely a concern during this type of stalking, it is possible for you to have one, two, or even more companions along to share your experiences. There are many possibilities in choosing a field companion. You may take along a more expert observer and learn from your companion; you may take along someone at about the same stage of development as yourself and share enthusiasm for new discoveries; you may take along a novice and enjoy the satisfaction of introducing someone else to the pleasures of wildlife observation, knowing that the introduction is, in effect, a gift, a gift of lifelong pleasure and good health. We who love and value nature must remember that one of the best ways to safeguard it is to teach future generations to love it also. This is best done in the field, not through books.

Whole parties can go on basic stalking expeditions—I have been out in groups of as many as twenty-four people. My experience, however, suggests that when a party grows beyond four people, difficulties arise. First of all, animals rarely allow a large group of people to approach as close as they would allow an individual or a small party. Consequently most sightings must be viewed at a greater distance. There is also the problem of communicating to a large number of people the whereabouts of a tiny animal somewhere in the distance. It's fairly easy for someone to use an arm and finger to point out something to people who can stand just behind his shoulder; but there's no way twenty people can stand just behind his shoulder at any one time. If you undertake to lead a large group on an outing you should expect these problems and be prepared to deal with the frustrations patiently and with understanding. In return, the number of eyes and ears in the group will almost certainly locate some unusual species that you would not have seen if alone, and the camaraderie and fair number of sightings usually result in a good time for everyone.

Intermediate stalking

Most common goals: May include those described in the previous section, but most often the goal is viewing other, often larger, birds and mammals that are quite shy of humans.

Typical walking: Along remote roads, trails, cleared right-of-ways, and paths, but frequently the observer leaves these to travel cross-country.

Physical demands: Mild to strenuous, depending on terrain, weather conditions, and time spent in the field.

Special clothing required: Especially important is footgear, described below. Other clothing should be comfortable and appropriate for terrain and weather conditions; various degrees of camouflage may be desirable, as discussed later.

Equipment needed: Binoculars. In unfamiliar country a topographic map, compass, and possibly a first-aid kit and survival kit. Other equipment as desired.

Cautions: In hunting season in areas open to hunting, blaze-orange clothing is strongly recommended. If the area is unfamiliar to you, ask someone who knows about possible dangerous terrain features. Tell someone where you're going and when to expect you back.

In intermediate stalking you attempt to cross the boundary into your quarry's safety zone and remain undetected. Extreme close approach may not be the goal and in fact may not be achievable except by advanced techniques discussed in the next section. But the extreme wariness of the quarry, combined with its superior senses, makes even moderately close approach a very satisfying experience. By its very nature intermediate stalking is best suited to the person who likes working alone. It is possible for two advanced observers to develop sufficiently good teamwork to function essentially as one individual; but ordinarily, two may be considered the practical limit.

In intermediate stalking you move through your chosen area at practically a snail's pace. You hope to attract virtually no attention to yourself, to be no more noticeable than a shadow on the forest floor. Rarely, however, can an individual sustain this level of invisibility through an entire outing, though almost anyone can attain it for brief periods.

Success at this level depends upon a number of factors. Environmental circumstances are powerful determinants of success or failure, and a cardinal rule may be stated at the outset: don't attempt this kind of stalking in an unsuitable area. It is pointless to attempt to stalk in a place that offers no opportunity for concealment. It is equally pointless to walk through an otherwise suitable area after a light rain and subsequent freeze have converted the ground surface to hoarfrost and every footstep, no matter how careful, sounds as if it were made on a bed of crunchy breakfast cereal. Anyone can easily imagine other environmental circumstances that would make this kind of stalking difficult or impossible. Your own mental and physical conditions also have a strong bearing on success here; but they are also of general importance and so will be discussed later in a separate section. For the moment, we can go on to the equally important subject of footgear and clothing.

Footgear. Important for comfort, safety, and success in walking quietly. After a number of years of experimentation I have settled on three types, all manufactured and sold by L. L. Bean, Inc., Freeport, Me. 04033. (Bean will supply a catalog upon request.) I'll discuss Bean products, though similar models by other manufacturers would serve the same purposes. The most desirable shoe, environmental conditions permitting, is of the type Bean calls the Maine Hiking Shoe. This is a light (27 ounces per pair) ankle-high canvas shoe with a natural-crepe sole. The sole has a fairly good gripping surface, is cushiony beneath the feet, and has rolled edges that permit almost total silence in walking. I use these in warm weather in both dry and wet conditions. When wet they do not get heavy with water, have no tendency to fall off the feet, and dry quickly. In cold weather (with warm socks) they are equally good in dry conditions but are unsuitable for wet weather. Their one drawback: though ideal for silent walking, they do not offer enough protection for difficult, rocky terrain.

When protection is needed I use the Bean Moccasin Boot, a short leather boot with a sturdy but flexible sole. When I first got mine about ten years ago (they were then called the Upland Hunting Boot) they were waterproof; but I've worn them so long now that the seams, though they can be sealed with dressing, soon begin to leak when subjected to protracted wetness. These boots are intermediate in weight (40 ounce per pair), very comfortable, and offer good protection to soles and ankles on rocky or treacherous ground.

For inclement weather I use a nine-inch-high boot called the Maine Hunting Shoe that is equipped with Vibram lug soles. The boots have an excellent seal between the rubber bottoms and leather tops, and given reasonable treatment with waterproof dressing, mine have so far been completely watertight. The Vibram soles make them quite heavy (about 56 ounces per pair) but I consider the trade-off worthwhile in exchange for the improved traction. The soles dig into and grip snow and mud (which many regular boot soles do not) and also seem to get fair traction on wet rocks and even ice, though ice is always a hazard without metal crampons. The Vibram soles also offer excellent protection from rock bruises. To me their only real disadvantage, since I don't mind their weight, is their tendency to bring mud, snow, and rocks into one's house. The easiest solution is to clean them outside with a brisk spraying from a faucet or garden hose.

These last two models of boots, I should add, permit reasonably quiet stalking. For circumstances where quietness is critical, a significant advantage can be gained by slipping oversize heavy socks over the outside of the boots. These serve to muffle footfalls and render almost any boot nearly as quiet as the Maine Hiking Shoe.

Clothing. Unless blaze-orange clothing must be worn, the stalker's clothing should be a color that blends into the surroundings. A camouflage pattern is helpful but by no means necessary, since animals react to movement, not form. It is possible, however, that a camouflage pattern helps lower the visibility of slight, slow movements, though I have not been able to determine this with certainty. Camouflage clothing is available at most sporting-goods stores and comes in a variety of hues and patterns. Choose one that blends well with the surroundings where you will be stalking. Especially important: clothing should be soft so that when you brush against limbs or twigs or the pant legs rub together as you walk the cloth will not make a whistling noise.

Head and face camouflage. If the stalker is moving through dark surroundings, the contrast created by a light-skinned face or hand makes any movement especially noticeable. Hands can be darkened with gloves; the face can be darkened either by camouflage creams or a head net. I have used the creams produced by the Bear archery company and find them very satisfactory. A kit contains three tubes, one each of green, brown, and black. The most effective way to apply the cream is to imitate the tricolored irregular pattern of camouflage cloth. A headnet is better suited to eyeglass wearers than to nonwearers because the glasses prevent the netting from coming into contact with eyelashes and sensitive eye surfaces. The net also reduces surface reflections from the eyeglasses and thus makes them much less noticeable.

Raingear. The aftereffects of rain create ideal stalking conditions. The same may be said of a light rain in progress. Vegetation underfoot no longer crunches and crackles; the air is usually still and does not waft odors about; and no direct sunlight falls upon the stalker to make his movements more visible. In warm weather a stalker may prefer to do without raingear and simply get wet. In cold weather, however, such a procedure can be very uncomfortable and raingear is desirable. I prefer a rain suit to ponchos and cagoules because a suit is less apt than the latter two to brush against and snag on branches. I use a camouflage rain parka and pants from Eddie Bauer, 3rd and Virginia, Seattle, Wash. 98130. (Bauer will supply a catalog upon request.) The suit is light, flexible even in extreme cold, and "breathes" so that body moisture evaporates away instead of collecting inside. There is a small amount of whistle when pieces of the cloth are rubbed together or when a tree limb brushes by, but the noise seems much less than with some other suits I have tried.

The stalker's walk. A successful stalker must learn to walk in a special way. Normal walking is designed for efficiency: its purpose is to get us from point A to point B in the most direct manner, usually along a straight line. The stalker's walk, by contrast, may get him from point A to point B, but seldom along a straight line. A stalker carefully avoids stepping on any substance that might create noise—dry leaves, twigs or limbs, gravel, loose shale, etc. He also avoids thickets or entanglements that would impede him and call attention to him if he had to break limbs, bend branches or small shrubs, or pull at tree-climbing vines in order to make a passage. Ordinarily, then, a stalker usually spends much time in sidestepping, stepping over, circling around, and even doubling back on his own path in order to choose a better route. Obviously he will work most efficiently if he pauses frequently and carefully studies out the best route to follow. But there is seldom a perfect route; he must learn to deal with what is available.

As he walks, the stalker uses his eyes to help him place his footsteps for silence. However, he cannot concentrate his full attention on this because he should be looking around at the environment, watching for his quarry. As he gains experience he will learn to use his peripheral vision and almost without conscious effort his eyes, though directed elsewhere, will help in picking out the best spot for a step. He also uses his sense of touch in making a choice. A good stalker "reads" the ground with his leading foot before placing his weight on that foot. If he detects a twig or chuckhole that might cause noise or movement if he stepped forward, he stops, visually examines the ground immediately in front of him, and either chooses a better site for the next footstep or backs up and chooses a new path.

Accomplishing this requires a radically different form of body control than that used in normal walking.

In a normal walk, steps are rhythmical and the body's center of gravity is typically slightly forward of the trailing foot. The effect is that the body is actually falling forward under its own momentum, though the fall is always checked and caught up by the leading foot, which then becomes the trailing foot as the body's center of gravity progresses over it with the forward stride of the opposite foot. The developed momentum carries the body easily and smoothly along. In stalking, however, this forward momentum is carefully avoided. The stalker keeps his weight balanced on his trailing foot until a safe placement has been found for the leading foot; only then does he shift his weight smoothly forward, where it is balanced on that foot until a new forward placement has been found for the opposite foot. The ideal is to be able to freeze at any point in the process and remain in the same position for several minutes without any difficulty in maintaining balance.

In comparison to a normal walk, a good stalking technique also requires different ways of using the legs and feet. In normal walking the knees of the trailing leg may be straight; but in stalking the knee of the trailing leg, in order to allow for the proper placement of the forward foot, must be slightly bent. In normal walking the forward foot may "slap" against the ground, but in stalking the initial contact with the ground is made only by the back edge of the heel, and then, as the body's weight swings forward onto that foot, the stalker "rolls" the footprint onto the ground, letting contact develop between the sole and the ground in a smooth progression from heel to toe. This minimizes noise and also disguises what noise is made by making it sound less like the rhythmical stepping of an ordinary walk. (A really good stalker can use this technique to walk across dry leaves and produce no discernible stepping noises, but only an uninterrupted sizzling sound as the soles of his feet roll continuously and smoothly from heel to toe. This achieve-

Strong sunlight falling on you creates a rim-lighting ef-fect that is highly visible when you are viewed from the shadow side because the rim-light contrasts sharply with your silhouette. You are least visible if you stay entirely in shadows.

ment, however, requires good physical condition, a fine sense of balance, and practice.) Needless to say, a stalker always raises his foot high off the ground for each stride in order to avoid striking his toes against obstructions. A person who develops this habit will not only achieve greater quietness, but also will seldom if ever trip or fall while walking through woods and fields.

Forward progress while stalking will of necessity be very slow. A good stalker, in fact, often spends more time standing still, intently looking and listening, than he does walking. Ordinarily, an individual selects a target area through which he wishes to stalk; in moving to the target area he walks in a more normal fashion until he is close enough to be seen and heard from the perimeters of the area, and only then does he begin his slow stalking technique.

Just as important as how you walk, of course, is where you walk. Try to follow the rules below:

1. Avoid being silhouetted against the sky. This is perhaps the most visible position you can be in. If walking on high ground to scan for quarry below, walk beneath the crest of the ridge, not on it.

2. Stay in shadows. Strong sunlight from any angle makes you more visible, but perhaps the worst is direct sunlight falling on your back. This creates a brilliant rimlighting that contrasts sharply with your main silhouette, the result being that any movement causes glinting effects that appear to magnify the movement in both extent and rapidity.

3. Often the best concealment is achieved by placing yourself in front of a tree, rock, or other object rather than behind it. If behind it, you must often move to peer around it in order to see your quarry; if in front of it you not only have a better field of view, but if your clothing blends into the background fairly well and you can remain motionless, there is little chance of your being visually detected except at extremely close range.

4. If you accidentally make a noise, immediately freeze. A noise will cause shy animals within hearing to stop their normal activities and focus their attention in your direction. While in this attitude they are most likely to detect you by any of their senses. Remain perfectly still until the animals have time to relax their attention and resume their normal behavior.

5. Don't let your equipment give you away. Check your binoculars, camera, or whatever else you're carrying for shiny sur-

This photograph illustrates that your image is considerably darkened if you stand in shadows (the effect is somewhat heightened here by the nature of photographic film). But two errors have been deliberately introduced. First, the subject is standing in front of a light background, which only serves to heighten his visibility; against a dark background his standing in shadows would have provided effective concealment. Second, the subject is letting light fall directly upon the reflective surfaces of his equipment. Such reflections are usually quite brilliant and can be seen from miles away. Reflective surfaces should be kept in shadows or, even better, covered with tape, cloth, or matte paint.

faces. Minimize reflections with cloth, tape, or flat paint. Often a pocket will contain a knife, film canister, loose change, keys, etc. If they make noise while you walk, figure out a solution. Some suggestions: separate the items; roll them in separate layers of a handkerchief; tape them together with masking tape. Avoid treating your equipment with cleaners or lubricants that have strong odors if your quarry has a good sense of smell.

6. Minimize your own chances of being detected by scent. Avoid the use of anything that produces a strong odor. Examples: dry-cleaning fluids in clothes; certain soaps; after-shave; cologne; medicated rubs and powders; cough drops; mints; chewing gum; certain foods (onions, garlic); certain drinks (liquor, beer); certain mouthwashes. Though these scents may not frighten an animal, they will cause all of its attention to be focused in your direction.

Making friends with wild animals. One of the delights of intermediate stalking is the opportunity to "make friends" with a particular animal. This is not always possible, but sometimes it can be accomplished by moving undetected into the creature's normal safety zone and then allowing the animal to become aware of your presence without frightening it. The best procedure is to assume a posture or attitude that suggests you are absorbed in and preoccupied with something other than the animal under observation. Make yourself as unintimidating as possible by eliminating quick movements, noises, and head-on gazes. With luck, when the animal detects your presence it will not flee; as seconds mount to minutes, it may gradually accept your presence and eventually seem unconcerned about it except to keep a wary eye in your direction. When you decide you have observed enough, withdraw slowly from the animal, still trying to appear unintimidating. The next time you encounter this individual animal it should be less fearful if it recognizes you as the same person. (You can help the animal recognize you by wearing the same or similar clothes.) After a series of such encounters, you will be able to approach the individual fairly closely even as it watches you if you keep your movements subdued and slow. You will be able to detect signs of nervousness which will indicate that you have about reached the limit of approach it will allow. In time you may come to know the animal and its range quite well and be able to find and observe it almost at will.

One of my recent lucky finds was a Cooper's hawk that eventually accepted my presence. This was a valuable find because these hawks are extremely high-strung, shy, and elusive, and observation of their habits is very difficult. I managed to approach within forty yards of the bird one morning, and while it seemed preoccupied with something in another direction, I began moving with painful slowness to seat myself on the ground. I had averted my face, and after I was seated was almost afraid to turn my eyes to see if the bird had flown; but it had not. So I stared at my feet for a while, at the same time raising my binoculars very, very slowly to my face. After what seemed like several minutes I finally positioned myself to look at the bird through binoculars. It was perched contentedly on a limb and occasionally turned its burning red eyes in my direction, but otherwise it seemed relaxed. It had evidently just fed, for its crop was full, and it appeared to be doing nothing more than resting. I watched it for almost an hour, during which time I gradually resumed more normal movements and postures. Finally I backtracked away, crouching low and moving slowly. Thereafter I learned the range and habits of the hawk and saw it almost every day, in similar circumstances, and within a week it would allow me to stalk to within twenty yards of it without showing any concern at all. I never tried to approach closer, for there was no need for me to do so—I could observe it quite well from that distance.

Unfortunately the bird met an untimely end. As I watched it one day it flew off its perch and in a few seconds I heard a small bird screaming. Thinking that it had caught a meal near the edge of an open stand of hardwoods, I decided to stalk through some pines to the edge of the hardwoods and watch the hawk at its dinner. When I got to my objective, however, a barred owl flew up from behind a log near where I thought the hawk should be. I sat down and observed the owl for several minutes; the whole time it watched me intently, and finally flew away. I moved closer to the log from which it had flown and found the Cooper's hawk still warm, but quite dead. My hypothesis is that the hawk caught a bird, and the owl was attracted by the bird's screams and attacked the preoccupied hawk from behind. An autopsy performed by Jerry Via, a Ph.D. candidate in ornithology, confirmed that the hawk was indeed killed by the owl—there were several talon punctures on the hawk's back and one wing had been broken by the blow of the attack. The lethal wound appeared to be a talon puncture through the right lung that caused a massive hemorrhage. A display skin was made of the hawk, and it is now in a collection of American bird skins owned by a museum in Kenya, Africa.

Careful stalking enables one to observe not only animals, but also the drama of life and death that unfolds constantly in the natural world.

Advanced stalking

Most common goals: Extreme close approach to shy birds or mammals that ordinarily the observer first locates at a considerable distance.

Typical walking: Remote areas; any type of terrain or habitat where the species is to be found.

Physical demands: Moderate to extreme, depending upon terrain, weather, and other conditions.

Special clothing required: Clothing of a color and hue that blends into the surroundings is almost essential. All-purpose footgear appropriate to terrain, weather, and stalking conditions.

Equipment needed: Good binoculars a necessity. For unfamiliar areas, compass and topographic map or, even better, recent aerial photos. In remote areas, first-aid and survival kits.

Cautions: Can be extremely dangerous in hunted areas during open hunting season.

In advanced stalking the observer attempts to penetrate deep into the safety zone of a shy animal and get close enough, say, to obtain good photographs with a camera equipped with only a moderate telephoto lens. The range must be quite close. Typical quarries might be white-tailed deer resting in a mixed deciduous-pine forest in the eastern United States; a flock of the western race of the wild turkey, *Meleagris gallopavo merriami,* grazing above the treeline in the Colorado Rockies; a puma feeding on a deer carcass in southwestern Texas; a goshawk at its nest in a Canadian conifer forest. To succeed, you must approach without ever being detected by any of the animal's senses—an accomplishment that demands the utmost in knowledge, skill, patience, and physical and emotional stamina. In the most critical stages of the approach it is not uncommon for a newcomer to the game to break out in a sweat and uncontrollable trembling, so great is the tension and emotional strain. Advanced stalking is not for the clumsy, the nervous, or the faint of heart.

The actual process usually begins when you first sight your quarry from a considerable distance with the aid of binoculars. Sometimes a more powerful spotting scope is used to pick up details not otherwise visible. At this point, you must study the quarry to determine what it is doing. Is it feeding? Resting? Actively hunting? Moving from one part of its range to another? Occupying a breeding territory? Escaping from a pursuer? These and similar questions must be answered before a realistic plan of approach can be made. Obviously, advanced stalking has one primary requirement: *The stalker must have a detailed knowledge of the habitat requirements and behavior patterns of his quarry.* If he cannot determine what the animal is doing when it is sighted, he cannot predict what it will be doing in the next few minutes or hours, or where it will be. Accurate prediction on these points is essential, because during most of the approach you will not be able to see the quarry.

If it seems possible to predict the animal's whereabouts, then an approach route can be planned. There are two possibilities. The first, and easiest, is that the quarry is moving along a predictable course. You then move behind concealment to a point along the animal's course, position yourself, and wait for the animal to arrive, and, you hope, pass within very close range. This is not as difficult as it may sound if the animal is following a trail, stream bed, old road, or other topographical feature; or if it is foraging or grazing along a strip of vegetation. You need only to find a route that will conceal you from the quarry's eyes, ears, and nose and take you to a suitable interception point. The best concealment is provided by landforms (ridges, the banks of dry streambeds, ravines) or by thick vegetation (a heavy growth of shrubs, a stand of young conifers). Many times you must be in excellent physical condition to traverse the route in time to reach the interception point sufficiently in advance of the quarry. Once at the interception point, you essentially utilize whatever possibilities for camouflage or concealment are available and await the quarry. Since you can remain motionless you have a very good chance of escaping visual detection.

The second and more difficult possibility is that the quarry is likely to remain fixed in one position. Your job then is to determine if a route exists that will conceal you from the quarry's eyes, ears, and nose and take you to within the desired range. You may have to rely on binoculars, topographic maps, or aerial photos to determine this. If there is such a route you begin the approach, making no attempt to see the quarry again until the last few yards, which are the most critical, for you are now deep within the animal's safety zone. You should attempt to be silent and invisible throughout the approach; and during the last few yards, if you can see the animal, you can gain an advantage if you move only when it is preoccupied with eating, putting on a mating display, or whatever else it may be doing. Every opportunity for concealment should be utilized during this final stage.

Many times, however, an approach route that provides adequate concealment simply does not exist. You then have to make a difficult choice between two alternatives. Should you abandon this quarry and search for another one in a better situation? Or should you attempt the most difficult stalk of all, a final approach where concealing cover is either inadequate or nonexistent? If you make the first choice, there is nothing more to be said. If you make the second, there is not much more to be said, either. You must accept the fact that your chances for success are very, very low. If you go ahead with the effort, however, there are two possible ploys that may help some.

1. Use the quarry's own behavior as a screen for the approach. Move only when the animal is preoccupied; freeze when it appears to be sensing the environment. This is probably the best method of open stalking, and often it succeeds quite well. I have walked up to within a few yards, sometimes a few feet, of a variety of animals this way.

2. Try to freeze the animal. This is extremely chancey. The best bet is to let the quarry become aware of your presence in such a way that it believes it has not yet been detected. Probably the best way is to let the animal see you walking slowly across its field of vision at an oblique angle as though you were going to walk right past it. Avoid looking at the animal and try to appear relaxed and natural, even preoccupied with examining the vegetation or the clouds. The animal may well flee; but there is some chance that it will decide to make itself as inconspicuous as possible and freeze. If it does, you can then

try to alter your line of progression so that it takes you to within the desired range; but you must continue to give the animal the impression that you are unaware of its presence. This can be tedious and nerve-wracking beyond belief, because the slightest false or sudden move will probably bring your game to an abrupt end.

By a seeming contradiction, there is an alternative to the oblique approach, and that is a full-front, head-on approach utilizing a special walking technique. A possible analogy is found in the glide approach of an attacking hawk. If the hawk sets its wings and glides directly into an observer's line of vision without any visible lateral or vertical movements, a kind of optical illusion develops in which, for a time, the observer is unable to gauge the hawk's distance—it simply looms larger and larger against the background but appears to be motionless. A falconer can observe this illusion easily when a hawk glides to the fist, and since many hawks use this glide tactic when approaching stationary quarry, presumably the quarry suffers the same illusion. A human walking can only approximate this illusion, but apparently can create it to some extent by eliminating all lateral movements of his legs and body and keeping his arms and hands still as he walks quietly and efficiently directly toward the quarry. Strangely, sometimes it works; but in my experience, it is impossible to predict in advance whether the quarry will remain frozen or turn tail as soon as the attempt is begun.

It doesn't need to be said that advanced stalking is much more of an art than a science, and aside from the rudimentary ground rules just mentioned, very little can be added that would be generally useful. Some people have very good luck in their stalking attempts, while others, who try just as hard and are just as well informed, have no luck at all. I'm at a loss to explain fully the reasons for this. I would, however, venture one guess. The more experience you've had in the wild and the more you feel at home out there, and the more you know about the species that you are attempting to stalk, the greater are your chances of success.

STILL-HUNTING

Most common goals: Seeing whatever animals live in or pass through an area; waiting at a good site for a particular species to appear.

Typical walking: Cross-country into suitably quiet areas free from human intrusion.

Physical demands: Usually mild, unless terrain leading into the area is difficult.

Special clothing required: None. Clothing should be comfortable and appropriate for terrain and weather conditions. The still-hunter's visibility is lessened if he wears clothing that blends into the surroundings, increased if he wears blaze orange. In either case, the real secret to success is stillness, not the color of clothing.

Equipment needed: Binoculars. A comfortable seat is necessary and may be created on the spot or carried in from outside. Other equipment as desired.

Cautions: Blaze-orange clothing is recommended during hunting season, especially when moving into or out of the area.

A good still-hunter gets to see a lot of animals he might never see by other methods, some at very close range. But watching a good still-hunter at work is only slightly more exciting than watching a rock. You might have to hold a mirror in front of his nose to tell if he's breathing. You might have to sight along a dead tree limb to tell whether he's really raising his binoculars. I heard of one fellow who was so patient that spiders anchored webs on his sleeves, wrens built a nest under his hat and started a family, vines ran up his legs to his knees, and moss started to grow on his north side.

No doubt very few still-hunters have so distinguished themselves. But all good still-hunters have one characteristic in common: a capacity for the protracted "stillness of posture" mentioned in the earlier quotation from Eliot Porter. If you sit still long enough, the animals that detected your presence by sight or hearing forget that you're there; and the scent molecules which you set free by moving into the area tend to drift away or decompose, leaving very few traces of your odor. You become, as far as the animals are concerned, just another inanimate feature of the landscape. Sometimes preoccupied small birds and mammals walk right over your feet and never notice.

But stillness of posture is not easily achieved. To understand the difficulties involved it is necessary first to understand that to a wakeful person, movement is far more natural than stillness. Most people have a compulsion to keep some part of the body—a hand, say, or a foot—in motion most of the time. An illustration. I once took a companion into the woods and left him at a good site with a comfortable seat, explaining the necessity for him to remain motionless. I went farther up the woods road and seated myself in a thicket of pines where I had a good field of view and could also see my companion, who, because of the way he was seated, could not see me. He was evidently making an effort to remain still—at least he kept the same seat and kept his back pressed firmly against a tree—but every few seconds he would turn his head, or shuffle one or the other foot, or raise a hand to scratch his head, or drum his fingers against his knees. Once he stood up very slowly, stretched, and sat back down. Except for this once he never moved the trunk of his body, but kept his head, hands, and feet in almost constant motion. He may as well have been waving a flag as far as many of the keen-eyed denizens of the forest were concerned.

When we left I asked him if he had found it difficult to sit still for so long. "No," he replied. "I stood up once to stretch, but other than that, I never moved a muscle." He was not lying. Like most people untrained in the art of stillness, he was simply not conscious that he had been making movements with his head, hands, and feet the whole time. Success in being still requires concentration and practice and comes only with effort—but, fortunately, not a very great effort. Most people can learn very readily to remain perfectly still for periods of up to an hour or so.

Of course it is impossible for anyone to remain motionless for a period of several hours. Even good still-hunters move from time to time. All their movements, however, are painfully slow and are made when no animals are nearby to be frightened by the movements and sound the alarm to others. However, it is possible to move without frightening an animal by the following procedure. Recently I had a deer walk to within about thirty yards while I was still-hunting. I began to move my binoculars very, very slowly; the deer obviously saw the motion and looked in my direction. I froze; the deer gazed at me for perhaps a minute, then looked away. Again I raised the binoculars, ever so slowly. The deer looked in my direction again. Again I froze.

Finally the deer began browsing on low-growing shrubs, and I continued moving the binoculars until I had them in position and could study the deer at leisure. So the rule is simple: move slowly; freeze under a direct gaze. The procedure is likely to work better with mammals than with the keener-eyed birds. You can accomplish the same thing, of course, by moving only when the quarry is behind a tree or other obstacle to vision. Quick movements are then possible, but are disastrous if the quarry unexpectedly emerges into view and sees the motion.

If an observer hopes to remain still for any length of time he must be comfortable. His clothing should be suitable for the temperature and loose enough not to bind or cut off circulation. He should avoid being hungry or uncomfortably stuffed with food or drink. If insects are abroad, he should use a combination of netting and repellent to avoid having to slap at things that crawl or bite. One of the most essential items is a comfortable seat. My father at age sixty-seven has had a lot of experience at still-hunting, and here describes two types of seats that provide comfort:

Procure a piece of polyfoam about 1½ inches thick and about 12×18 inches; and one piece of lightweight, waterproof tarp or plastic about 4×6 feet. Fold the tarp to a convenient size and roll the polyfoam tightly inside. Then tie each end of a light cord, long enough to form a shoulder strap, to each end of the roll. This device is easy to carry, makes a soft waterproof cushion, serves as a ground cloth, and can serve as a rain-protector or blanket in an emergency.

Another type of seat can be made from a 5-gallon plastic pail. Make a lid by cutting a piece of ½-inch plywood slightly larger than the top of the pail. On the underside of the lid fasten wooden blocks 1 inch thick so the lid will fit snugly and remain in place. The top of the lid can be covered with polyfoam and upholstered to make a comfortable seat. The pail will hold lunch, thermos, raingear, and a lot of other items as well. Paint to blend with natural surroundings.

I personally prefer the pail seat to the commercially available folding stools because I have never yet sat on a stool that one or two of its legs didn't sink into the ground. A pail, of course, does not have this problem, and, being larger, also carries more gear than can be stuffed into the pocket of a folding stool. This is particularly important when you are carrying a lot of equipment, as when photographing from a blind. If you wish to travel light, it is always possible to find a seat on a log, stump, or rock; but usually, unless dragged to the foot of a tree, these seats do not provide a backrest, nor do they provide a background to break up your silhouette. A solution is to carry a convenient size of plastic sheet to form a waterproof seat on the ground at the base of a large tree or rock. The backrest thus provided is a real comfort during periods of prolonged stillness, and the background breaks up one's outline very nicely.

Anyone planning to still-hunt for a long period—say one whole day—should devote some advance thinking to three problems: food, drink, and bodily wastes. Obviously, the first and last meals of the day can be taken before going to and after leaving the still-hunting site. It is the midday meal and other snacks that create a problem. Eating necessitates movement, makes noise, and releases a number of food odors into the air. Opening a thermos of hot coffee is a particularly good way to release strong odors. The question the observer must answer is this: "Should I eat here and release all these odors? Or should I eat elsewhere and create a disturbance getting there and back?" If birds are the quarry, the odors don't much matter; but with mammals the situation is very different, since any strange smell will put them on the alert. I prefer to eat elsewhere if I'm still-hunting for mammals, and to take the meal at midday, which is normally a quiet period for most animals. While away from the hunting site you can also take care of any bodily waste problems without contaminating the still-hunting area with odors. If you must urinate or defecate near a mammal still-hunting area, you should bury the waste beneath four to six inches of soil to mimimize the characteristic human odors that can alert mammals for many yards around. You can minimize the problem to some extent by curtailing your liquid intake before and during the still-hunting period.

Still-hunting is naturally most effective in an area where animals move freely about, and the considerations in choosing a site are discussed in a subsequent section, "Choosing and Using a Territory." Time of day is also important. Diurnal birds and mammals tend to feed, drink, groom, and play in the early morning and late afternoon and to loaf and rest at midday. A good still-hunter times his activities around those of his quarry so that he is most still and quiet just when they are most active.

Still-hunting is not everybody's cup of tea. Some people are too restless and fidgety to be comfortable at it, and I hesitate to say how many times I've walked up on still-hunters in the woods sound asleep. It is also a chancy business. I've spent an entire day in a place and seen nothing interesting, whereas the day before in the same place I had watched a veritable parade of animals go through. However, for those with suitable temperaments, still-hunting can be an excellent way to discover what animals use an area and to watch them going about their business undisturbed by the observer's presence.

IV

CHOOSING AND USING A TERRITORY

There are two great pleasures for the wildlife enthusiast. One is going into new territory. The other is returning to a home territory that is known in complete, intimate detail.

New territory is unknown, exciting, filled with the promise of new animals and new experiences. It is a place for exploration and discovery. Later the memory recalls the single visit as a series of photographs of the landscape, showing the peculiarities of the light and the horizons and what the trees and vegetation were like, and if it was a good trip one remembers too the beauty of some animal seen during an intense moment of discovery. New territory is a change of scene, a new combination of earth and water and living things, and one needs it every so often and comes away from it refreshed in body and spirit.

But for comfort and inner peace one turns to the easy familiarity and old friends of a home territory—the path worn by one's own feet, the favorite tree, the special seat by a secluded stream, the cheerful call of quail, the hawk soaring lazily in the sun, the deer who raises her young in the thicket every year, the rabbits who emerge into the clearing at dusk, the owl that calls from the forest before dawn. It is a landscape known in all its guises—in the misty morning rains and tentative greens of spring, in the dense foliage of July, in the hazy air and mellow colors of autumn, in the iron cold and clear starlight of a winter's night. It is a place where the seasonal traditions are known; where the comings and goings of flowers and birds and mammals are linked in the mind with the length of the days and the shifting temperature; where the weather is so intimately known that changes in the barometric pressure register in the mind like sounds too faint almost for hearing; where, one might speculate, it would be good to be buried someday and somehow feel the passage above of the wind and days and clouds and seasons forever. Home, in the old phrase, is where the heart is, and those whose only homes are inside houses are the sad casualties of our technological culture.

It is true, of course, that a single visit to an area can be pleasant and memorable and that on such a trip one can see a lot of good wildlife. But glimpsing an animal once does not compare with knowing the creature well, any more than meeting a new person once at a cocktail party compares with a close friendship of many years' standing. As one learns his home area well, he comes to know the animals intimately. He learns the breeding territory of the buck deer, the boundaries marked by "scrapes" in the fall; the nesting territories of songbirds, their boundaries proclaimed by song during spring and summer; he knows a dozen entranceways to underground tunnels or tree hollows where tiny mammals raise their young, and a score of birds' nests and the number of eggs in each. With experience he comes to know every animal as an individual, with a territory, appearance, and "personality" uniquely its own. As he learns a creature's habits through the seasons, he may be able to find the individual animal, with fair reliability, at any given time on any given day it is in residence. In short, he will have established a personal, one-to-one relationship with the animals. The quality of this experience is much greater than the sum of its parts, and, like love, is difficult to describe, perhaps because it is itself an experience of love.

What characteristics make an area suitable for regular visits? For the beginner or even the experienced person with interests in the whole spectrum of a wildlife community, a good answer to that question is, "An area with diverse habitats." A habitat, in simple terms, is a place that meets a species' requirements for food, water, and cover (shelter). Some species, for example, prefer to live among mature trees; others prefer thick, brushy areas; others, open fields; still others need streams or open water. The list could be extended indefinitely.

The greatest abundance of wildlife is usually found where two different types of habitat join to form a habitat boundary, or edge. The increase in wildlife along the edge is sometimes spoken of as the "edge effect," but ecologists do not agree on terminology, nor do they agree on how to account for the phenomenon. But basically it works this way. Say for example that you have a hardwood forest adjoining an open, grassy field. Using birds as an illustration, if an observer walked a quarter-mile through the woods he might see ten species; walking a quarter-mile in the grassy field he might encounter four species. But by walking a quarter-mile along the edge between the woods and field he might encounter sixteen species—the ten species he found in the woods, the four he found in the field, plus two additional species that typically inhabit a forest-field edge. The edge effect seems to hold for mammals, insects, and other classes of living things as well as for birds.

If we recognize that by joining different habitats in different combinations we create a whole range of edges, then it becomes clear why we place value on a territory with a variety of different habitats: in part it is also because it has a number and variety of edges. In central Virginia where I live, a good area would include a lake, a marsh, a stream, a hardwood tract, a pine tract, a brushy field, a grassy field with hedgerows, and perhaps still other zones all adjoining in a number of combinations. For several years, in fact, I lived only fifty yards or so from just such an area and walked through it almost daily.

An important consideration in choosing a home territory is that it be easily accessible. People who live in rural areas have ideal situations because most are within walking distance of a variety of wildlife habitats. Suburbanites in many cities also live near large undeveloped tracts that make good territories for viewing small birds and mammals. True urbanites usually have to travel to a park or to undeveloped land outside the city. It is seldom necessary to drive long distances, however; public wildlands or parks are now established near almost all urban areas. Convenient accessibility is so important that if given the choice between an excellent area ten miles away and a fair-to-good area within walking distance of my home, I would choose the closer one because chances are I would spend more time there, know the animals better, and enjoy it a lot more.

Identifying the wildlife in an area

Having chosen a site for regular visits, the user will want to identify the birds, mammals, and perhaps other forms of animal or plant life found there. The seasoned naturalist working in a familiar region will of course have little trouble in making identifications, but the beginner, or even the advanced naturalist working in an unfamiliar region, will want to own one or more regional field guides to identification—pocket-sized books that use a combination of illustrations and text to point out the distinguishing field marks of separate species. (The advanced student may want more complete scientific volumes, but these are generally too bulky and too detailed for the beginning naturalist to carry in the field.) Field guides to birds, mammals, flowering plants, and numerous other groups of wildlife are listed in the bibliography at the end of the book.

In using field guides, beginners will greatly improve the accuracy of their identifications if they pay particular attention to the ranges of the species they are working with. Range maps or descriptions usually accompany each entry. Checklists of local or regional species are also valuable aids to accuracy. Good sources of published checklists are nearby bird clubs or ornithological societies, state or province fish and game commissions, and the biology departments of regional colleges or universities.

But sight records of birds and mammals are not the only

means of determining which species inhabit an area. Birds especially may be identified by their calls and songs. Recordings that identify many natural sounds are also listed in the bibliography, as are field guides that enable one to identify animals by their tracks. Predators can sometimes be identified by the remains of their kills, and an experienced naturalist is often able to make identifications on the evidence of molted feathers, tufts of fur, droppings, castings, diggings, borings, scrapings, and various other bits of evidence usually overlooked by the casual observer.

Reading the landscape

Another benefit of close familiarity with a diversified home territory is that one learns to associate each species with a specific set of habitat conditions. As a very obvious illustration, in my section of the country we associate upland hardwood forests with squirrels, turkeys, great horned owls, and Cooper's hawks. When the trees are harvested and the area is open with perhaps a few dead trees left standing, we look for rabbit, quail, barn owls, and red-tailed hawks. As immature second-growth trees appear we expect to find deer, grouse, screech owls, and sharp-shinned hawks. In mature hardwoods that are moist and somewhat swampy we look for beaver, woodcock, barred owls, and red-shouldered hawks. But beyond these easy and rather obvious associations are refinements and more refinements as one learns about the habitat preferences of more and more species. Eventually one acquires the ability to look at a landscape and forecast in great detail the composition of the differing wildlife communities that will be found within different zones of the landscape. This ability is a source of pleasure as well as a useful tool for the investigative naturalist. It is also a means of mystifying novices who, not understanding how such forecasts are made, are likely to conclude that the forecaster must possess some occult power of divination.

Keeping lists

Most naturalists keep a written record, or "life list," of all the species they have correctly identified. Separate lists are kept for members of different biological classes—birds, mammals, flowering plants, etc. It is important that any entries on the lists be accurate—that is, that the species identification be unquestionably correct. Most list-keepers also observe the following rules. First, the recorder himself must make the identification; he may seek the help or counsel of others more familiar with the species, but he himself must perceive the features that distinguish the specimen from all other species. Second, the specimen must be observed in a live, natural state. Captive, domesticated, or dead specimens do not qualify for entry on a life list.

List-keeping sounds dull to many people who have not tried it, but actually it is great fun if done in a proper, simple fashion. A life list provides the compiler with a reflection of his own experience, and he can take pride and pleasure in knowing that as the list grows, so does his expertise as a naturalist. Life-listing quickly becomes an enjoyable competitive game, with points going to the individual with the largest lists, since they are considered evidence of success in finding and identifying species. Birders in particular are avid listers, and one of the most prestigious accomplishments of North American birding, as mentioned, is to qualify for membership in the 600 Club.

The life list is only one type, however, and others provide equal enjoyment. The following types will add not only pleasure, but also scientific value to the observations one is able to make on his own home territory.

The area list records all the species an individual is able to find within a strictly defined area. The area itself can be anything the compiler wants it to be. For a bird list it could be a very small area around a feeder, a back yard, a strip of woodland, a farm, a mountain, a valley, a stretch of beach, or any similar unit. Some birders keep several area lists, each for a differently defined area such as a back yard, county, or state. But it is the list for the home territory which is visited regularly that provides the greatest potential for enjoyment and value. Such a list will include not only the species encountered, but significant dates: the arrival and departure dates of migratory birds, the dates when birds lay eggs, the dates when mammals bring young out of their dens, the dates for the blossoming and fruiting of plants, or anything else of interest to the observer. These records provide the compiler with a picture of the annual cycle and a "schedule of coming events" for subsequent years. Such a list, constantly updated, grows increasingly pleasurable and valuable as the years go by.

The census list is also of interest. It is an annual or semi-annual record of a home territory. In this, the compiler attempts to list as accurately as possible the numbers of individuals of each species. The census should be conducted on or near the same date each year. Popular times are the Christmas holidays; the peak of the spring breeding season; and late summer, when populations are often at their highest for the year. As the census figures accumulate from year to year and population changes become apparent, questions emerge that lead one into fascinating avenues of thought and investigation. Pondering the reasons behind the changes, one begins to see the complex interrelationships between a living creature and its environment, the subtle, far-reaching influence that a change in the weather or a change in a food supply may have on the entire web of living creatures whose livelihoods are all somehow interconnected. Such firsthand knowledge of ecology is invaluable, for it is much more immediate than knowledge gained from reading.

A daily list is often kept by many birders of the species seen on their home areas. The accumulated data provide a good picture of population changes, activity levels, migratory movements, etc.; a wealth of meaningful conclusions can be extracted by an alert analyst.

A trip list is a record of the species encountered during a journey. The exact locations of rare or unusual sightings are recorded. The list serves not only to help in remembering the trip, but also as a guide to places where rare species might be found by other interested parties.

List-keeping is something most naturalists do by choice, and it can and should be fun, not work. But if records are accurately maintained over a period of time, they can have significant scientific value. A simple list of breeding robins on the University of Michigan campus prompted an investigation into the reasons for their declining numbers, which in turn led to the discovery of the deleterious effect of DDT and other chlorinated hydrocarbons, the writing of Rachel Carson's *Silent Spring*, and finally the eleventh-hour ban on the use of these pesticides, which, if their use had continued, could have caused a disaster of enormous proportions to the earth's biosphere. It is entirely conceivable that a similar list kept by someone else might someday have the same value.

Learning about animals

Most people who are curious about wild animals are also curious to know more about them than can be learned from direct but limited observation. The ideal way to gain additional knowledge is through reading. Readable, interesting accounts of individual species can be found in the following:

GENERAL

For bird lovers:	Bent, Arthur Cleveland. *Life Histories of North American Birds,* 26 volumes. New York: Dover Publications, Inc. (paperback reprints).
For mammal lovers:	Cahalane, Victor H. *Mammals of North America.* New York: The Macmillan Co., 1961.
For hunters and photographers:	Elman, Robert, and George Peper, eds. *Hunting America's Game Animals & Birds.* New York: Winchester Press, 1975.

REGIONAL

Most states and provinces have books entitled *The Birds of . . .* (state or province) and *The Mammals of . . .* (state or province).

SPECIFIC

Many species of birds and mammals have been the subject of separate books. Consult your local library's subject file in the card catalogues.

Becoming a specialist

There are so many birds and mammals that a person cannot hope to learn all there is to know about all of them. Most people who are interested in wild animals soon select a family, genus, or species for special study. This step is best taken only after the person has already become a competent generalist and has at least a nodding acquaintance with most of the species in his area, for only then can he understand how his special quarry functions within the context of its environment.

Most specialties probably develop out of a person's natural affinity for and interest in a certain kind of animal. The usual process is that the person becomes fascinated by a creature as a result of having some experience with it in the wild. He then begins reading all he can find about his subject and seeking out as many individuals as possible for further observation and study. He soon locates all the appropriate habitat for the species within a certain radius of his home, conducts a census of his quarry within these areas, learns the territories of many of the individuals, and perhaps selects two or three pair for intensive study.

In studying his quarry the serious naturalist will want to compare his own findings with the information in the published literature on the species. He may learn that his own insights are significant, new, and worthy of publication in an appropriate journal. There are many standard questions asked about every species, such as: What precise elements define its preferred habitat? How large is its territory? How does it claim and defend its territory? What are the critical elements of its breeding displays and patterns? How does it prepare its offspring for independent existence? What are its significant communication signals? What is the species' major food supply? What are its major enemies? What are its longevity and mortality figures? When, why, and how does it interact with other species? How does it affect its environment? For a number of species, questions such as these have been answered only partially, tentatively, or not at all. Even for those species whose life histories have been thoroughly documented, newly formulated questions arising from the ethological and ecological sciences provide a steadily increasing need for new investigations and new information.

Undoubtedly most amateur naturalists begin developing a specialty without any intention of ever publishing their findings. Many, of course, do not discover anything new; their pleasure comes from the fact that experience and knowledge gained firsthand in the field is its own sufficient reward. Those who do make new discoveries, however, may have the added pleasure of sharing their findings with others through the medium of the printed page.

V

OUR EYES AND OPTICAL AIDS

Compared to a hawk's eyes, human eyes are pitifully weak, and over half of the adult human population have deficient vision even by human standards. Many wildlife observers wear corrective lenses; all of us must use binoculars and telescopes if we wish to see details of wild birds and mammals at normal viewing distances. These optical aids are vital to the process of observation, for they make the difference, literally, between seeing or not seeing at the full capacity of one's eyesight. Eyeglasses, binoculars, and telescopes all come in a variety of shapes, styles, and models, some suited for wildlife observation and some not so suited. The following sections attempt to discuss eye use and what experienced observers feel are the most important features to look for in optical aids.

OUR EYES

Good eye care begins with good general health care. Our eyes function best when we are in good overall health and may begin to suffer if we are in poor health. Vision may deteriorate rapidly as a side effect of diabetes, vitamin deficiencies, and other physical disorders. In addition, there are specific diseases of the eyes, such as cataracts and glaucoma. When I discussed the matter of eye care with several doctors I got pretty much the same answer in each case: Have a thorough physical examination once a year and an eye examination every two years; but if sudden problems or rapid changes occur in vision, see an ophthalmologist immediately and describe the symptoms fully. Quick action is important because some kinds of eye deteriorations are irreversible and result in permanent damage even if the causative disease is cured.

Getting the most from our eyes outdoors

Good wildlife observers use two visual techniques outdoors that ordinarily are not needed or used very much indoors. Both techniques are normal visual functions, but most beginners who are unaccustomed to searching for animals in the wild have to learn the techniques through practice. Neither is difficult.

The first technique involves making the greatest possible use of peripheral vision. An attempt is made to see a large segment of the environment at a glance so that one's surroundings can be scanned quickly, with only a few movements of the head and eyes. To accomplish this, mental attention is directed to the image transmitted by the entire retina rather than to the clearest area in the center. The act is often described as "looking at everything and nothing at the same time." Using peripheral vision is a technique for locating animals and features of the environment that one wishes to study more closely. For close study, the second technique is employed. Peripheral vision is ignored and mental attention is focused on the small area of sharpest vision transmitted by the fovea. An attempt is made to see the finest possible details. A person who can do this is often described as a "keen observer" or a "trained observer."

There are often amazing differences between the observations of those who have mastered these techniques and those who have not. Take two people out birding, one who is an experienced observer and one who is not. Both have 20/20 vision. They are walking through a mixed hardwood-coniferous forest. The first observer suddenly points upward. "There's a bird," he says. "Where?" says the second observer, who was walking right beside the first and had the same field of view. The first shows it to him. "Oh, yeah," says the second, and looks at it through binoculars. The bird flies away. "Well," says the first, "what did you see?"

"I don't know. It was just a bird."

"Now think," says the first. "It had a blue-gray head, an olive-brown back and wings, very prominent white wing bars, a clear white throat and underside, and prominent white spectacles. Now what was it?"

"I don't know. I didn't see all that stuff."

"Okay. Those are the field marks for the eastern race of the solitary vireo." He takes out a field guide and shows his companion the illustration. "The best thing to look for is the very big, very prominent white line around the eye that makes it look like it's wearing spectacles."

The first of these observers used his peripheral vision to locate a bird that the second was not aware of. He then concentrated on seeing details while the second saw only the gross image of "bird." The first observer, however, is getting the second one started on the road to seeing by emphasizing one detail out of many that the beginner can concentrate on. The next time the beginner encounters a similar bird with prominent white spectacles he may exclaim, "Solitary vireo!" and feel an absolute flush of pride. Of course he may or may not be correct in his identification, for other species also have white spectacles; but at least he's beginning to see details and associate them with a species, and so should be encouraged. With practice, he'll get better and better. Someday people may speak of him with admiration, saying he's an "excellent" birder. What they will mean is that he has learned to see excellently.

Protective eyeglasses

Today I have about 20/10 vision in my left eye and somewhat less, between 20/10 and 20/15, in my right eye because of mild astigmatism. I do not wear corrective lenses. But I would probably be blind in my right eye if I had not been wearing protective glasses while firing an international competition rifle course at the Army's Marksmanship Training Unit (MTU) at Fort Benning, Georgia, several years ago. A .308 cartridge ruptured and sent a stream of hot gases, burning powder, and metal fragments through the bolt directly toward my right eye. Fortunately I was wearing shooting glasses and escaped injury, but since then another young man disobeyed instructions, did not wear his glasses, and because of a similar accident had his right eye so badly injured that it had to be removed. The number of accidents at the MTU is extremely small. Millions of rounds are fired there every year by the best marksmen in the world, using the best equipment available. Only one such accident may occur every several years, and then only as a result of equipment failure. But when it does, an eye may be lost, and the loss is permanent. Equipment does fail, without warning. Bits of debris and even ballistic projectiles may ricochet about and send rock or dust fragments flying. I never fire a gun of any kind any more without wearing protective glasses. I urge everyone else to do the same.

I also wear protective glasses when I must walk rapidly through thick brushy areas, which often occurs when I go out hawking or when I'm carrying a heavy, bulky load of photographic equipment through such an area and have both hands occupied. In either situation the chances of getting slapped across the face by a limb or other vegetation are pretty high. The right kind of glasses provide good protection to the sensitive eye tissue. I use Bausch & Lomb Ray-Ban shooting glasses, for three reasons. First, the lenses are very large and thus interfere only minimally with peripheral vision. Second, the optical quality of the glass is good and the lenses are virtually free of distortion. Third, the glass is tempered to withstand the impact of a 5/8-inch steel ball dropped from a height of fifty inches. The glass is not unbreakable, but it is strong. The large lenses are comfortable to wear and filter out ultraviolet rays that cause eye fatigue. Ultraviolet light is abundant around large bodies of water, snow, and sand, and at high altitudes.

Shooting glasses should be worn to protect the eyes from the severe damage that can result from firearm equipment failure. Most models can be supplied with lenses that are clear or tinted with gray, green, or amber.

Corrective eyeglasses

A majority of adults wear corrective lenses, so I discussed the subject with several of my acquaintances who wear them and are also quite expert in wildlife observation. Only one wore contact lenses, and he said that any problems he had with them while watching wildlife were problems which he ordinarily had anyway, and those were minimal. He liked them and recommended them. Dr. Porter Echols, Jr., my ophthalmologist, agreed that, for the person who can wear them comfortably, contact lenses are probably very well suited for wildlife observation since they interfere very little either with peripheral vision or with the use of binoculars.

Two of my sources are past retirement age and are experts in various phases of wildlife. One is my father, a casual birder and an expert hunter. I have hunted with him for years and though in latter years he has worn corrective glasses I have seen no diminution in his ability to see wildlife nor in his sometimes almost incredible marksmanship with fast-moving targets. He ordinarily wears trifocals, but recommends bifocals for the hunter and has written these comments:

Ordinary bifocals or trifocals create a problem when you're walking in the woods because you must tilt your head way forward in order to see over the near-focus part of the lens and get a good look at the path near your feet. The problem is solved if you use shooting glasses with large, pear-shaped lenses. If the near-focus section is ground into the lowest portion of the lens, you do not need to tilt your head very far in order to see the ground near your feet; and by merely looking downward at close objects you have good near vision without having to carry a second pair of glasses.

I also prefer Ray-Ban glasses. The large lenses provide good peripheral vision and do not obstruct your view when you put your face against a gunstock to sight along the barrel. Prescription lenses can be obtained in either glass or plastic. The plastic is strong, and lighter in weight than glass by about 50 percent; with good care, it should remain clear for years.

My other source is Mrs. Myriam P. Moore, one of the most expert birders in my acquaintance. A grandmother and recently retired from the U.S. Selective Service with extraordinary recognition for outstanding service to the nation, Myriam has for years used her considerable administrative skills to organize large-scale bird-population studies in central Virginia, including annual hawk-migration studies along the Blue Ridge. At the same time that Barry Kinzie and I were determining the greatest distance at which we could see hawks, we noticed that though there were ten or twelve good observers at the site, Myriam consistently detected more distant hawks than did all the rest of the observers together. She too wears trifocals and feels they are well suited for most birding activities except relatively advanced stalking, though a person wearing bifocals or trifocals for the first time, she says, must expect some frustrations until he becomes accustomed to the different portions of the lenses. Beyond that, she thinks the greatest concern with eyeglasses outdoors derives from the effects of weather. Here are her comments:

Your readers may find it hard to believe, but you and I know that excitement mounts fast when an observer becomes aware or even suspects that he is about to focus on a rare bird or on the private life of a timid wild creature. In cold weather, warm breath is sure to fog over your glasses at the critical moment if you're not careful. This delicate mist is as impenetrable to the eye as a solid wall, so the trick is to remember (if you can!) to keep your mouth closed and to exhale forcefully enough to prevent the warm breath from rising onto your glasses. Since it's easy to forget these things in an exciting moment, however, it's a good idea to keep a soft, absorbent cloth such as a clean cotton handkerchief close at hand for a quick, adroit wipe—otherwise you may miss the show altogether. Binoculars also fog easily in cold weather. Because cold objects collect mist more readily than warm ones, it's helpful to keep your binoculars warm by letting them hang inside your coat when they're not in use.

In warm weather glasses may require wiping if they fog from either perspiration or rain. Rain-spatter on glasses is a problem in any season and is best prevented by a wide-brimmed hat—until you look up! Then the handkerchief must be brought out again.

Wearers of bifocal or trifocal glasses are often cautioned against scratching the surfaces of these expensive lenses. In my experience it has proved safe enough to hold my binoculars directly against my eyeglasses if the binoculars are fitted with adjustable rubber eyecups. Users of binoculars with metal eyecups may find it necessary, as one birder did, to cushion the rims of the cups with strips of Dr. Scholl's moleskin corn pads.

One final word. Still-hunters and stalkers should be aware that the surfaces of eyeglass lenses reflect both sunlight and skylight and thus can be visible for miles. A wide hat brim is the best way to prevent these reflections. A headnet is also useful for the same purpose.

BINOCULARS

Good binoculars are indispensable aids to viewing wildlife, and anyone who wishes to do most of the things described in this book needs a serviceable pair. If you own a pair and are satisfied with them, you may wish to skip over the technical parts of this section. But if you are thinking of buying a pair for yourself or someone else, the somewhat technical discussions are designed to save you money and help prevent disappointments. They attempt to explain why binoculars may cost anywhere from a few to several hundred dollars; what you may expect from models in the various price ranges; what features you may need for general- or special-purpose viewing; where to buy binoculars and obtain repair services; and how to care for and use binoculars for the best results. I have tried to cover each of these topics with reasonable thoroughness because most people who use binoculars have questions about them from time to time but have difficulty finding adequate answers.

The usefulness of binoculars

Binoculars—often called "glasses" by their users—are useful tools that help us find, identify, and study birds and mammals in the wild. Viewing almost any habitat through binoculars will reveal animals that would not have been detected with the unaided eye. Binoculars also permit accurate identification by species, both of the creatures that will not permit close approach, and of those that will permit close approach but have such small identifying marks that unaided visual identification is impossible or at best uncertain. Binoculars enable us to study animals at a distance without disturbing their normal behavior, and to more easily locate bird nests and mammal dens for detailed life-history studies. They are useful aids in stalking and tracking. It is difficult to imagine anyone who needs to see wildlife for any purpose who could not be aided to some degree by binoculars.

But binoculars have a value beyond simple utility. All healthy wild birds and mammals are beautiful, and binoculars reveal details of form and nuances of color that we would otherwise miss. For most people, viewing these details is a highly pleasurable experience. Almost anyone who has looked through binoculars at the eyes of a great horned owl, or the color of a fox's brush, or the astonishing details of a great blue heron's nuptial plumage will never again want to look at wildlife without binoculars. Seen through them, even the most familiar creatures become objects of delight and hold the onlooker almost spellbound. On an all-day field trip it is not unusual for me and my companions to spend several hours looking through binoculars, often at species we know well; but we continue to look because seeing detail and beauty is, to the naturalist, one of the most fundamental and most intense of pleasures.

Pitfalls in buying binoculars

The sales of binoculars in the United States indicate that many people appreciate their value; the advertising and selling of binoculars is now a multimillion-dollar industry. Unfortunately this has led many manufacturers to enter the competition by offering low-priced glasses that are poor in quality and often defeat, rather than aid, the viewer's purposes. Sometimes the poor quality is evident at a glance; in other instances it may be concealed beneath a handsome exterior. The binoculars may seem quite good when examined in a store, and may perform satisfactorily in the field for a time, but then quickly deteriorate. Then there are more subtle flaws which cannot be detected except by careful attention. For example, I once owned two inexpensive models produced by different manufacturers. One clear spring day I was looking through one pair at a small bird perched on a power line about a hundred yards away. I thought it was an eastern bluebird, and I could easily see the blue on the bird's back; but since it should have been a mature bird and since I was seeing it from the side, I should also have been able to see the red on its breast. Try as I might, I could not. Puzzled, I looked at the bird through the other pair of binoculars. This time I could easily see the red, but the blue had become a nondescript, colorless gray. The one pair of binoculars transmitted blue effectively, but not red; and with the other pair the situation was reversed. Further comparison of the two binoculars showed them to be severely flawed in revealing the true colors of small objects viewed at a distance. Such a flaw is subtle, but significant. The effects are poor image quality and confusion in the mind of the viewer.

Binoculars may prove unsatisfactory in three different ways: the optical quality may be poor; the mechanical parts may be inadequate or unsuited for a given purpose; or the size, weight, and balance may make the binoculars uncomfortable or difficult to use. Cheap binoculars almost always fall short on at least one of these points. Occasionally expensive models do. When it comes to making a choice between inexpensive and expensive models, however, there are two schools of thought. One is the "throwaway" school which holds that any pair of binoculars will sooner or later be damaged in the field and that in the long run it is cheaper and more convenient to buy inexpensive binoculars and simply throw them away as they get damaged, rather than bother with expensive and time-consuming repairs. The other is the "quality" school which holds that with reasonable care a good pair of binoculars will last for many years and, though initially more expensive, is ultimately less expensive than a series of cheap binoculars with predictably short life-spans. There is some merit to either position. For a long time I was a member of the throwaway school, but later I began using binoculars for long periods each day and began to suffer eyestrain from the flaws in the optics. So I decided to buy a pair with high quality. I'm glad I did, for they virtually eliminated the eyestrain and provided great viewing pleasure, but I'm not sure the price would make them the best buy for only occasional, light use. Whichever school you join, you will find an array of models to choose from.

How do you make a good selection from among the hundreds of models offered for sale? The best way is to acquire knowledge about how binoculars work and what various features can be built into them. Then decide what particular combination of features you need, based on the purposes for which you intend to use the glasses. This is a vital step, because no one pair of binoculars is ideally suited for all purposes, and glasses of excellent quality may perform a given function very poorly, if at all. The next step is to make a tentative selection of a brand and model, or perhaps two or three comparable ones. Here you try to achieve a satisfactory balance between the features you desire and the limitations of your budget. You may have to trade off a bit on one or the other. The next step is perhaps the most important: Test the binoculars by using them in the field to see if they meet *your* needs and expectations. Even the most scrupulously honest sales literature cannot reveal whether the glasses will suit your personal tastes when you use them for your purposes.

A field test can be arranged in two ways. One way is to buy the binoculars with the understanding that you may return them for a refund after a short trial period. Be sure, however, to have this stated in writing on the sales slip. Another way is to borrow the same model from a friend. If he has subjected the glasses to much use, he will probably be able to give you reliable information about how they perform, their shortcomings, etc. There is another advantage to borrowing from a friend: you are thus free of an obligation to a particular dealer and may then ethically shop anywhere for the purpose of comparing prices. Often considerable sums can be saved by purchasing from discount dealers who have good prices but are unwilling to sell on a trial basis. Reputable dealers of both types are listed in the later section on dealers and repair services.

How binoculars work

An important first step to understanding how binoculars work is to clear away the confusion that exists in advertising. Manufacturers of inexpensive binoculars often advertise their models by means of a chart using two columns to compare the features of their model with another brand costing much more. The comparisons are usually based on numerical values such as power, lens diameters, field of view, weight, and so forth. Such a chart may mislead the buyer to conclude that he is getting a $50 model that is in every way comparable to a $500 model. But this is seldom, if ever, the case.

Most comparison charts used in advertising are based on quantitative measurements only and fail completely to indicate the *qualitative* measurements which are much more important, but difficult to state in layman's terms. The quality of a pair of binoculars resides in the optical formula of its lens system and in the mechanical construction of the housings, and both of these are significantly affected by manufacturing and assembly techniques. Let's look first at how a lens system operates, and then look at the various quantitative and mechanical features that can be built into a pair of binoculars. We will then be able to discuss what combination of features makes a pair of binoculars suitable for a given purpose.

The lens system. The *raison d'être* of any pair of glasses is its lens system. There are two basic types. In one type, properly called *field glasses,* a system incorporating only two simple lens groups is employed in each barrel. Based on an optical formula used by Galileo, these instruments cannot readily achieve a magnifying power higher than 4× or 5× and have very small fields of view. Nowadays such a system is employed most frequently in inexpensive opera glasses.

This cutaway model reveals the three lens groups found in most prism binoculars. This model employs a roof prism which eliminates the "hips" found in the more commonly seen design, but the basic function of the optical groups is the same in all prism binoculars. (Photo courtesy Carl Zeiss, Inc.)

Much better for our purposes are the second type, the so-called *prism binoculars* that incorporate a series of several glass elements in each barrel. The elements are variously shaped with concave, convex, or flat surfaces and are arranged in groups. Some of the elements are separated by air spaces, and some are joined by special optical cements. Prism binoculars usually employ three major groups of elements: the objective or image-forming group, found in the front of the barrel, produces a magnified and reversed image; the prism group, found near the midpoint of the barrel, folds the light path and reverses the image again so the user sees a normal view; and the ocular group, found in the eyepiece, allows the user to change the focal point of the system and adjust the eyepiece to variations in his own eyes. The ocular group is important also because its design determines the width of the field of view and controls many factors that contribute to image quality.

Designing and manufacturing an optical system demands extreme precision. The designer of the system starts by setting certain goals, such as power and field of view, and then begins the complex problem of computing the light-bending or refractive qualities of the lens elements he will need to achieve his goal. The complexity arises from the light-bending qualities of the glass, or rather types of glass, that he can use. There are many types of optical glass available to him, each with different chemical and physical properties. Each type differs from all others in light-bending power; that is, if identically shaped and curved elements were made from different types of glass, each would bend light rays to a slightly different degree. This quality is called the glass's *refractive index,* and can be stated mathematically. Each type also has its own *dispersion index,* also statable mathematically, which indicates the degree to which it separates or disperses the focal point of short (blue) and long (red) wavelengths of light by bending them at differing angles.

No known type of glass bends all wavelengths of light equally. As a result, a single lens of significant power will not bring both long and short wavelengths into focus on the same plane. The result, for a viewer looking through the lens, is an unsharp or fuzzy image, often with aberrant color fringes around the edges. Additionally, the curvatures of some lens elements introduce distortions when an object is viewed through an edge of the lens—the image may appear elongated, compressed, or bent. In designing an optical system, one of the designer's primary goals is to "correct the aberrations" introduced by the refractive and dispersion indices of the lenses and their curvatures. By choosing various types of glass with different indices, and grinding their surfaces in different ways, he can cause some elements to cancel out the aberrations introduced by other elements. So developing a good optical formula is achieved only through lengthy and complex computations.

A perfectly corrected lens system of the type used in binoculars is not possible, though the designer can, through greater and greater refinements of his computations, approach close to this goal. New technology may someday make the perfect system possible. But for now, lens systems are best described in terms of the degree of correction built into them. A highly corrected system, though not perfect, nevertheless provides a crisp image, is relatively free of distortion, and performs well across the entire field of view. A less well-corrected system provides softer, less detailed images, or distortions, or both; and generally its best performance will be limited to the very center of the field of view.

Designing a lens system used to be a time-consuming operation involving months of working with complex mathematical formulae. Now, however, modern computers can perform the computations within a matter of minutes or hours. But computers do not perform magic, and in themselves do not guarantee perfectly corrected lens systems. All the computer does is to follow directions given to it by the programmer. The computer can be programmed to formulate a lens system within given parameters, including materials and assembly costs. The computer accepts the basic data fed into it, cycles through the computations several times in order to refine the mathematical statements, and stops when it has satisfied the requirements of the program. The program may require almost any degree of optical correction. Computers have significantly reduced the cost of lens-system design, and a number of manufacturers have taken advantage of them to formulate lens systems that are quite good.

But mathematical precision alone does not guarantee good optical performance, for overall quality is strongly affected by manufacturing techniques. The types of glass employed in the system must, from the molten state, be free of physical and chemical impurities, and of air bubbles. Each element must be accurately ground and polished—an exacting process—and perhaps coated to reduce reflections. And then all the elements must be firmly and precisely aligned in the binocular barrels, free of dust and scratches. If they are not precisely aligned or "centered," the curvatures of the various elements will work against one another to produce distorted images. The problem is compounded because both barrels must be precisely matched and balanced for magnification, brightness, and focus in order to produce identical images—otherwise the user may experience severe eyestrain and fatigue. Often the differences in price between inexpensive and expensive binoculars reflect the differences in the manufacturing care and the cost of skilled labor required to achieve good assembly.

Since the whole purpose of binoculars is to produce a magnified, clear image, the lens system is the most important feature—but not the only important one. Many other features help determine quality and the purpose for which the binoculars may be used. Let's look at some of those now.

Magnification. Binoculars are usually described by a pair of numbers such as 7×35 and 10×40. The first number of the pair specifies the magnifying power, and the second the diameter of the front (objective) lens expressed in millimeters. Thus 7×35 refers to a 7-power glass with a 35mm objective lens; 10×40 to a 10-power glass with a 40mm objective lens. Binoculars are commonly available in powers ranging from 6 to 20. One of the first questions a prospective buyer asks is, "What power binoculars should I buy?" The answer depends on how and for what purpose he intends to use the glasses. The basic principle to keep in mind is that the power of a glass magnifies two things equally: the object being viewed; and any tremors imparted to the glass by the viewer's hands. The higher the power, the more the view seems to bounce around before the viewer's eyes, and at powers of 12 or more the glasses become virtually useless as hand-held instruments.

Almost everyone who has experience with binoculars agrees that the most suitable powers for general viewing are 6×, 7×, and 8×. These powers are great enough to be really useful, for they make a distant object seem approximately only 1/6, 1/7, or 1/8 as far away. Yet most people can hand-hold a glass of these powers steady enough so that the image does not seem to be dancing violently around in the field of view. A very few people can hand-hold 10× glasses steady enough for clear viewing, but most cannot. I can hold *some* 10× glasses steady enough to see small details, but the effort and concentration needed to do so are too great to permit prolonged viewing comfort. Since I enjoy looking through binoculars and do so a great deal, I use models that I can look through comfortably—7× or 8×. There are other advantages to these powers that will be discussed later.

Objective lens and exit-pupil. The size of the front or objective lens determines two things: the amount of light entering the barrel, and the size of the exit-pupil. The exit-pupil determines the diameter of the beam of light emerging from the eyepiece. If the exit-pupil is small, only a narrow beam of light strikes the viewer's eye; if the exit-pupil is larger, a correspondingly larger beam strikes the eye. If the binoculars are honestly made, the size of the exit-pupil is easily determined: divide the size of the objective lens (in millimeters) by the magnifying power. Thus a 7×35 glass has an exit-pupil of 5mm (35 ÷ 7 = 5). A 7×50 glass has a 7.1 mm exit-pupil, and a 10 × 40 glass a 4mm exit-pupil.

What is the significance of exit-pupil size? For our purposes, it is simply this: If the exit-pupil of the glass is smaller than the pupil of the user's eye, the image he perceives will appear dimmed, as if the light intensity of the scene had been reduced. But, on the other hand, if the exit-pupil of the glass is larger than the pupil of the user's eye, the image he perceives will not appear any brighter than the scene appears to the unaided eye because the diameter of the beam of light entering his eye is then determined not by the exit-pupil of the glass, but by his own eye pupil.

In short, the size exit-pupil anyone needs is one that corresponds to the size of his own eye pupil under the viewing conditions he normally encounters. Eye-pupil size may vary from individual to individual, but averages under different light conditions as determined by a U.S. government study during World War II are as follows:

bright sunlight	2.5mm
heavy cloud cover	3.5mm
dusk	5.0mm
bright moonlight	6.5mm
complete darkness	7.0mm

For average daylight viewing, then, an exit-pupil of about 3.5 to 4.0mm is adequate. If a person does a great deal of viewing in conditions of dusk or deep shadows, he may gain an advantage by using binoculars with a large exit-pupil, such as a 7×50 or an 8×56. Such models are often called "night glasses." They are, however, about twice as heavy as a standard 7×35 model. Many people who use glasses under both conditions have two pair: a light, comfortable model for daytime use, and a heavier night glass for darker conditions. (There is one other advantage to a larger exit-pupil: in conditions where the viewer cannot hold a steady position, such as in a light boat on choppy seas, a large exit-pupil is some aid to maintaining the field of view if the eyecups tend to shift position in relation to the eyes. But this is not the same as hand tremor, in which only the front of the binoculars move while the eyecups remain unchanged against the viewer's face or eyeglasses.)

The eyepoint and eyecups. When the viewer's eyes are positioned behind binocular eyepieces so they perceive the entire field of view clearly and comfortably, they are said to be at the "eyepoint." This point is usually about 11mm behind the eyepieces. If the binoculars have metal eyecups, eyeglass wearers may be forced to position their eyes behind the eyepoint and consequently see only a tiny area of the binocular's field of view. This is a waste of the binoculars' usefulness, and besides is very frustrating. Of course the person can always remove his eyeglasses, but this too is frustrating. The best solution, now found in most models, is a pair of rubber eyecups which can be left up for those who don't wear glasses or folded down for those who do wear them. For those who don't wear glasses, rubber eyecups are also more comfortable than metal ones. If you are stuck with binoculars with metal eyecups, a competent binocular repair service can usually install rubber eyecups for a modest price.

Coating. Almost all modern binoculars have coated lens elements. On external surfaces, good-quality coating can be seen as a bluish or purplish tint when the surface is viewed from an angle. Applying an optical coating is not a simple process. It is accomplished by placing the elements in a vacuum chamber and vaporizing the coating material, usually magnesium fluoride, which then "blooms" on the surface of the lens. The process is often controlled by visual inspection. Since the process is an added expense, some manufacturers coat only the visible, external lens surfaces. In a good system, all necessary surfaces, including those inside the barrels, are coated.

Coating reduces reflection and thus improves light transmission through the system. An uncoated air-glass surface will reflect about 5 percent of the light striking it. Good coating reduces the amount of reflection to about 0.5 percent. So if an uncoated system contains ten air-glass surfaces, about 40 percent of the light will be lost, compared to only 5 percent in a well-coated system. (Not 50 percent for the former, as might appear at first glance: 0.95^{10} = about 0.60, though 0.995^{10} = about 0.95.) Coating thus makes a significant improvement in image brightness. It also has other effects. The light reflected from air-glass surfaces inside the system has to go somewhere, and it can start bouncing around from one surface to another, producing flare, or non-image-forming light. To the viewer, flare looks like a gray film appearing inside the lens system and results in image degradation. An uncoated system can produce so much flare when struck by direct sunlight that the image becomes almost useless. Proper coating will not eliminate flare entirely, but does usually reduce it to acceptable levels.

Twilight factor. Twilight factors are often touted by sales literature, but they are just meaningless numbers unless the lens system is good to begin with. The factor indicates how bright a scene will be rendered in dim light. The twilight factor is influenced by the power of the system as well as by the objective lens size. It is determined by taking the square root of the product of the magnifying power and the objective diameter. Thus for a 7×35 model, $\sqrt{7 \times 35}$ = 15.6; for an 8×30 model, $\sqrt{8 \times 30}$ = 15.5; for a 10×40 model, $\sqrt{10 \times 40}$ = 20. The higher the factor, the greater the efficiency of the binoculars in rendering details in dim light. (Some distributors substitute "relative light efficiency" for "twilight factor." This is computed by the same formula multiplied by 1.5, so that a pair of 10×40 binoculars is stated as having a relative light efficiency of 30.)

Field of view. The width of the viewing field seen through binoculars is usually expressed in units of width at 1,000 units of distance; for example, 130 meters at 1,000 meters, or 150 yards (or 450 feet) at 1,000 yards. Generally, the higher the magnifying power of the glasses, the smaller the field of view. A small field of view makes for difficulty in locating the object to be viewed. The field is determined primarily by the optical formula of the ocular lens group.

For general viewing, a moderately wide field of view is highly desirable. A few years ago, a standard field of view for 7× binoculars was considered to be about 360–380 feet. For higher powers it was considerably smaller. But even years ago good design could produce a 7× glass with field of view of about 450 feet, and modern computers and technology can now easily produce a wide-field formula. One "extra-wide field" 7× model is even advertised as having a field of 650 feet! But extreme wide-field views introduce optical aberrations unless produced by almost prohibitively expensive techniques.

I now use 7× and 8× glasses, both with fields of about 420 feet, and for me they are entirely adequate. It is important to note that all wide-field binoculars will have some image degradations around the edges of the field—usually cloudiness or distortion. In a good system, image degradation around the edges will be barely noticeable—in fact, you may have to look carefully to detect it. In a poor system, the degradation will be severe, will be a distraction, and probably indicates that the glasses will cause eyestrain during prolonged viewing.

Close-focusing distance. Binoculars have a fixed close-focusing distance, the minimum distance at which objects can be brought into clear focus. Objects closer to the observer than this distance cannot be viewed through the binoculars. Generally, lower-powered binoculars can be focused closer than higher-powered models, but, again, this depends greatly upon design and construction. In cheaper binoculars the close-focusing distance may vary considerably even among glasses of the same model produced by the same manufacturer.

Though a short close-focusing distance is not important to an observer who is interested only in viewing objects and scenes at a distance, it is a real advantage to the wildlife observer who wishes to see birds and mammals up close. Nothing is more frustrating than to maneuver carefully into position, only to find that the tiny creature you have stalked is in the "dead zone," too close for viewing with binoculars but too far away to be seen in detail by the unaided eye. If general-purpose glasses will focus no closer than eighteen or twenty feet, the dead zone will be considerable. A good 7× or 8× model for our purposes should focus to about twelve or fifteen feet. Some will focus even closer. A short close-focusing distance is also a valuable aid in tracking.

Close-focusing distance is to some extent determined by the focusing powers of the user's eyes. If two people are using the same pair of binoculars, one may be able to focus on closer objects than the other. On many models the close-focusing distance can be improved by a competent technician (but this should not be attempted by an amateur). However, the best bet is to buy binoculars with a good close-focusing distance to begin with.

Types of focusing. The focusing mechanisms on binoculars are of two general types: individual-focus (IF) and center-focus (CF). There are variations on the CF design. The type of focusing mechanism is important in determining whether or not a glass is suitable for a given purpose.

In the *individual-focus* type each barrel is focused separately. Focusing is accomplished by turning the eyepieces. Since there is no bridge connecting the two eyepieces, one of the weakest mechanical parts found in the center-focus design is effectively bypassed. Thus the IF design is inherently more rugged and also somewhat less expensive to produce. A further advantage of the IF design is the possibility of improved sealing against dust and moisture. Because the eyepieces revolve on threaded tubes rather than slide back and forth on smooth tubes, it is much easier to introduce a tight seal. Many IF models are advertised as dustproof and moistureproof, and some are hermetically sealed and filled with nitrogen to prevent internal fogging.

The IF design is best suited for applications where ruggedness and weatherproofing are important and where adjustment of the focus is seldom necessary. It is well suited for marine use and for use in stalking animals in mountainous country where rocky terrain, slippery footing, and uncertain weather conditions are the rule and where close viewing distances are seldom encountered. For wildlife observation under more ordinary conditions, however, the IF design has severe limitations. Focusing each eyepiece separately is slow and always requires the use of both hands, and considerable dexterity at that. If the animal is moving rapidly, or even slowly, either toward or away from the observer, it is often impossible to bring the animal into focus at all. Since in general viewing we are apt to encounter animals at almost any distance, and since most animals do move about a great deal, the CF design is much preferred for general use.

In the *center-focus* type both barrels are focused simultaneously. Focusing is usually accomplished by turning a wheel mounted on the hinge between the barrels. A variation is the so-called "rapid focus" mechanism which replaces the focusing wheel with a thumb-operated lever. In either case a practiced user can achieve almost split-second focus and can easily maintain focus on a moving animal. The CF design is thus ideally suited for general wildlife observation.

There are two types of CF designs: external-focus and internal-focus. The external-focus design is the most common. It works by means of a bridge that connects the focusing mechanism to both eyepieces. Turning the mechanism moves the bridge and causes the eyepieces to slide back and forth in unison on their tubes. The design is practical and relatively inexpensive, but it does have weaknesses—in fact, it is probably the weakest mechanical point in binoculars of this type. The weakness arises primarily from the necessity for the eyepieces to slide back and forth on tubes. Since they must slide easily, the fit of the eyepieces and the tubes must not be too tight; consequently the seal between the eyepieces and tubes is not perfect, and dust and moisture can work their way into the barrels. Moisture is particularly a problem when binoculars are worn around one's neck while sweaty from heat or exertion. The usual result is that condensation occurs inside the barrels, fogging the lenses and making the glasses useless until they can be dried out by heat or a draft of air.

Dust is more insidious, because once inside it can be removed only by disassembly, which requires the services of a technician. But perhaps the worst problem is that dust and grit may accumulate between the eyepieces and tubes at different rates for each barrel and create different degrees of friction. If this occurs and the bridge mechanism is weak, the eyepieces will not move in unison and the barrels will not focus at the same distance. The strength of the bridge can easily be tested by applying moderate forward pressure to the right eyepiece. If the bridge is weak, the right eyepiece will slide forward on its tube and the bridge will rock on the hinge post, causing the left eyepiece to slide backward on its tube. A bridge that is weak to begin with will almost certainly cause focusing problems unless the binoculars are well protected from dust and dirt, especially windblown sand. Among CF binoculars of the external-focus type, only the most well-designed and best-constructed (and most expensive) models are relatively immune to dust and moisture problems.

A second type of CF binoculars incorporates an internal focusing system. In this type the focusing wheel is connected by a precision gear system to movable elements inside the barrels, and the system allows for complete hermetic sealing of the barrels. In effect, the only moving external part is the focusing wheel itself. In many ways the design is ideal, but expensive to manufacture. True internal focusing is found only among the very finest and most costly binoculars.

Size, weight, balance. General-purpose binoculars should be a handy, comfortable size and weight. My personal standard is that they should not be much over twenty-four ounces. Most good 6×30, 7×35, and 8×30 glasses fall near or below this weight. The only real justification for a weight much above twenty-four ounces is to achieve some goal for which general-purpose glasses are not designed anyway, such as high magnification or a high twilight factor.

In my experience the balance or "feel" of a pair of binoculars is important in determining how steady they can be held. I suspect this is a very personal matter, probably based on the dimensions of the user's hands. A glass that feels right to one user will not necessarily be the first choice of another user. My only advice is that if you are shopping for binoculars, handle several different models that meet your other requirements. Probably some of these will feel better balanced than others, and you may be surprised at how much steadier you can hold the ones that feel "right."

Buying binoculars

Assuming that you want general-purpose binoculars, a bewildering variety of models and price ranges are available to you. Only you can decide exactly what you want and are willing to pay for, but an intelligent choice can save you a great deal of money and give you vastly greater viewing pleasure than you might otherwise get. A few special-purpose models will be mentioned later, but for now let's discuss center-focus models in the 6×, 7×, and 8× power range. For convenience of discussion the models have been divided into four price categories.

Under $50. Typically made in Japan and sold in the United States by chain stores and discount houses under their own brand names. The optical formulas of some of them are surprisingly good, but assembly of the lens system is frequently poor, resulting in extreme variations in optical quality among different glasses of the same model. Search through a number of the same model and buy one only if the optics are satisfactory. If they are flawed, they certainly aren't going to get any

The Mirakel Special 7 × 35 model is representative of modestly priced, general-purpose binoculars of external center-focus design.

better. Watch especially for loose elements (which will rattle if shaken), misalignment of the barrels, and mismatched brightness or magnification in the barrels. If the optics are satisfactory these inexpensive glasses can be perfectly adequate for people who will not subject them to hard use—for example, someone who spends times indoors watching birds at a yard feeder, or perhaps takes the glasses outdoors only occasionally on short walks in mild weather. They have a predictably short life-span under hard use, however, because their poor sealing will quickly admit dust and moisture; and one good jolt usually puts them out of commission by jarring loose the elements or breaking the bridge/focusing mechanism. This is normally the type of glass preferred by members of the "throwaway" school.

$50–$100. Typically sold under the manufacturer's own brand name. Most of the problems mentioned above apply to this class also, so shop warily. But you should have a better chance of finding satisfactory optical quality combined with more rugged mechanical construction, which makes this range more suitable for outdoor use if handled carefully. I own a model in this range and believe it to be an exceptional value. It is a "Mirakel Special" 7×35, manufactured in Japan but sold by the Mirakel Optical Co. Mirakel states that they personally inspect, adjust, and correct each "Special" model to their own rigid specifications. A good guarantee comes with the glass. I have not seen other glasses in the Mirakel line and so cannot vouch for them; but my glass compares favorably with many models I have seen in the next category, and in many such comparisons has actually been optically superior.

$100–$200. This is the class most observers "move up to" after going through two or three pairs of less expensive binoculars. Many purchasers in the "quality" school buy a model in this class to begin with. They are adequate for all but the most demanding use. There will be little variation in quality between glasses of the same model, so you can usually buy with confidence. Do not assume, however, that models in this class are indestructible. They are not. Dropping them in beach sand or giving them a hard jolt may necessitate costly repairs. In this class the well-known brands I have examined are the top-of-the-line models produced by Bausch & Lomb, Bushnell, and Nikon. There are differences among comparable models which might be important to the advanced observer—differences in features such as width of field of view, close-focusing distance, weight, size, and balance.

$400 and up. In this class are the so-called "ideal" binoculars produced, as far as I know, by only two firms: Ernst Leitz, Inc., and Carl Zeiss, Inc., both of West Germany. Both companies have been in existence for generations and are world-renowned for the quality of their optics. Many people dismiss their binoculars as being merely expensive status symbols, but this is a

misconception. Far from being expensive toys, the binoculars produced by these firms are true workhorses. They have very high optical correction, and a solid effort has been made to incorporate into them an ideal combination of features. Both manufacturers make several models (and Zeiss several types) of glasses supplied with lifetime guarantees against manufacturing defects. Similar models by both manufacturers compare favorably. Because I frequently use binoculars for several hours a day I finally bought a Zeiss model designated "8×30 B dialyt." My choice was based on very personal biases. First, NASA sent Zeiss optics to the moon, and I place great trust in NASA's quality-testing procedures. Second, the Zeiss was slightly smaller from the Leitz equivalent and I preferred its balance and feel. I have no complaints whatever about mine. They are remarkably handy and reveal details and color nuances that are not visible through lesser glasses. Of great value to me is the virtual absence of eyestrain even after prolonged use. Considering the quality and the unusual combination of features, glasses in this category are, in my opinion, a good value for anyone who needs or enjoys high-quality optics and subjects binoculars to prolonged use in conditions where dust, dirt, or moisture are hazards to ordinary glasses.

Special-Purpose Binoculars

Some wildlife observers have special requirements for binoculars because they do their viewing under unusual conditions. Following is a list of some common types of special-purpose models. Some have already been discussed briefly in the previous section.

Heavy-duty models. Discussed above. Essential features: extra-rugged housing with individual-focus design and hermetic sealing. Zeiss makes both individual and center-focus models with two armor coatings, an inner one of steel, an outer one of protective rubber.

Dim-light models. Discussed above. Essential features: a large exit-pupil (6mm or 7mm in diameter). High magnification produces a high twilight factor, also a consideration here.

Lightweight models. Often preferred by mountain climbers and backpackers who must count every ounce, and by a few general-purpose types who prefer the light weight. Typical models are 6×20 and 8×20. Quality ranges from "instant junk" to surprisingly good. Their usefulness is limited in dim light. Many glasses in this category are miniature in size and can be slipped into a shirt pocket for convenient carrying.

Zoom models. Zoom (variable-power) binoculars are available from a few manufacturers. Typical models are in the 7–12× power range. A major disadvantage arises from the difficulty of designing and manufacturing a simple power-control mechanism that will maintain an optical balance between the two barrels. In manual models this seems to be a very failure-prone feature. In battery-powered models the weakness can be mitigated somewhat, but at the expense of greatly increased bulk and weight. Other disadvantages include a reduction of image quality and often severe loss of brightness as the optics are racked to higher magnifications. Opinions vary on the value of this type of glass, but among the users I have talked with, some common evaluations did emerge. First, the zoom feature is seldom necessary or even useful in normal fieldwork, and the short life-span of the zoom mechanism makes this type a poor investment compared to the more reliable fixed-power type. Second, the zoom feature can serve as a substitute for a telescope when a scope is not available, but it is not a good substitute. A 20× scope has much greater magnifying and light-gathering power and consequently produces far more useful results. An ideal combination, most observers feel, is a pair of general-purpose binoculars and a 20× or higher-power scope. When this combination is impossible or impracticable, however, zoom binoculars may offer a compromise solution. The prospective buyer will have to weigh the advantages and disadvantages and be guided by his own judgment.

TELESCOPES

When an observer wants high magnification for extra-long-range viewing, a telescope is the ideal solution. A scope is not intended to be a hand-held instrument, so considerations of nice weight and balance do not apply to its design. Consequently a large objective lens can be employed to provide great light-gathering power that will yield a satisfactorily bright image at magnifications of 20×, 40×, and even higher. (The type of scope used for wildlife observation is the terrestrial telescope, often called a "spotting scope." Celestial telescopes designed for astronomy and draw-tube scopes of the type used in pirate movies are not suitable for our purposes.)

Many spotting scopes are built around 60mm objective lenses, and 20× is considered a standard power because it yields a 3mm exit-pupil and a bright image. At higher powers the exit-pupil diminishes and the scene appears considerably darkened. Also, higher powers tend to magnify the aberrations in the optical system so that image quality deteriorates. Nevertheless, it is possible to change the magnifying power of many spotting scopes. One system consists of interchangeable, fixed-power eyepieces of, say, 15×, 20×, 30×, 40×, and 60×. Another system involves a variable-power or zoom mechanism built into the body of the scope which racks from 15× to 60×. Still another consists of a variable-power eyepiece which racks from 20× to 45×. For the user who will need and use high powers of 40× or more a great deal, a model with a fixed-power eyepiece is preferred because the eyepiece can be fairly well corrected for aberrations. Variable-power optics, on the other hand, either will be well corrected for only one power (usually the lowest), or will be prohibitively expensive. The inexpensive variable-power mechanisms, however, may serve well enough for the user who only occasionally needs power above 20× and doesn't wish to bother with interchangeable lenses.

Users of telescopes should also be aware that viewing objects at great distances involves optical difficulties that arise from atmospheric conditions. Dust and moisture particles in the air tend to scatter light waves and diminish the vividness of color and sharpness of detail in a scene. The atmosphere is seldom if ever very clear of these particles. Another effect arises from the tendency of light rays to bend when they pass through media of different densities. When a familiar but complex combination of sunlight and air currents create irregular heat zones in the atmosphere, the variations in temperature create variations in the density of the air, and light rays passing through them are bent. The result, known popularly as "mirage" and scientifically as "schlieren effect," causes displacement, distortion, and a rippling effect in the image. The combined effects of scattering and bending light rays make it difficult to observe fine detail at long distances even with the best telescopes.

Because of its high magnification a telescope must be mounted on a tripod or some other base which allows for stability. Tripods are widely used, and with good reason: when closed a tripod is fairly small and maneuverable, yet when opened it positions the telescope at eye level and allows it to be aimed in almost any direction. The controls can be locked in position, freeing the user's hands and enabling him to move about or allow others to look through the scope. In my judgment only reasonably sturdy tripods should be used—lightweight models tend to vibrate in the slightest breeze and make viewing all but impossible. As a guide, the tripod should weigh between four and six pounds, but since the tripod's stability depends upon its design as well as its weight, these figures are only approximations. Tripods are sold in almost all photographic-supply shops.

An altogether different type of mount is a rifle stock. A gunstock is not a substitute or replacement for a tripod; rather, it is an alternative way of mounting a telescope when mobility and speed are more important than prolonged, leisurely viewing. If the gunstock is equipped with a sling, the apparatus can be carried behind the shoulders, is much less cumbersome than a tripod, and is especially handy in brushy terrain where a tripod always seems hell-bent on snagging everything within reach. A gunstock-mounted scope carried in the hands can be brought into use almost instantly, whereas setting up a tripod may require several seconds. A gunstock also provides an excellent way to use a telescope from inside an automobile.

Some people claim to be unable to hold a gunstock telescope steady enough for useful viewing in a free-standing position, though others have no trouble at all. Even so, most people who use a gunstock scope feel that 20× is about the upper limit of power that can be used in this position. To gain increased stability, the gunstock can be braced against a tree trunk or limb, automobile, fence post, building, large rock, or anything else that's suitable. Using a support often provides enough stability so that powers of 40× and higher can be used with ease. In the absence of external supports—as might occur on a beach, for instance—the gunstock user can increase stability by using the sling in a kneeling, sitting, or prone position.

Adjustable metal gunstocks designed for use with cameras are sold by some photographic supply houses. A suitable gunstock can be made by the home craftsman from a wooden blank, and discarded rifle stocks can frequently be bought from gunsmiths at reasonable prices.

A third method of using telescopes is perhaps worth mentioning. It consists simply of using the hands to clamp the telescope firmly against a tree trunk, car roof, or other support. This frequently involves assuming awkward and uncomfortable positions, but it does work in an emergency and provides a means of using a scope when you wish to travel especially light, without either tripod or gunstock.

The market is not as glutted with telescopes as it is with binoculars. While I'm aware of others, the brands that I'm most familiar with are Bausch & Lomb, Bushnell, and Swift. I have a particular fondness for the old Bausch & Lomb Balscope Sr., which I used for years on rifle ranges, but recently it has been manufactured in such small quantities as to be difficult to find. Many of my friends own and like another model, the Balscope Zoom, which has an internal variable-power feature ranging from 15× to 60×. I have used this model and it is, in my opinion, quite good. I presently own a Bushnell Spacemaster II model with a variable-power 20×–45× eyepiece. I chose the eyepiece after comparing it with fixed-power and wide-angle eyepieces, both 20×. At 20× the variable-power eyepiece was so well corrected that there was no detectable difference between it and the fixed-power model, but the wide-angle eyepiece produced noticeable pincushion distortion. The variable-power eyepiece seemed the best choice because it provided excellent correction at 20× and the option of going up to 45×, which is sometimes useful even though deterioration of image quality is very apparent. Image quality improves steadily as power is racked down toward 20×. Bausch & Lomb and Bushnell telescopes retail at prices ranging from slightly over $100 to near $250. Discount prices are often much lower.

Probably the ultimate in small telescopes is the Questar. It is American-made and incorporates a catadioptric system of mirrors and lenses that allows for small size and light weight, but great resolving and light-gathering power. Manufacturing quality controls are so high that most models actually exceed the theoretical limits of instrument resolution. A number of different eyepieces are available, providing magnifications up to 160× and beyond. I have borrowed and used Questars only briefly, but that was enough to convince me that they really are incomparable instruments. Though expensive (about $700 and up), they might nevertheless be a good investment for anyone who must use a telescope extensively or for critical purposes.

TIPS ON USING BINOCULARS
AND TELESCOPES

1. Practice. There is no substitute for acquiring the "feel" of a particular optical instrument. You should be able to focus automatically, without having to think of which way to turn the focusing mechanism. Practice picking out an object in the distance and raising your binoculars to your eyes and focusing on the object without ever losing sight of it. This, too, should become automatic.

2. Keep 'em clean. Just one little smudge on either end of an optical instrument can wreck image quality, and a tiny amount of grit on any moving part can spell disaster. Learn to clean properly. First, avoid rubbing optical-glass surfaces whenever possible since this wears away the optical coating and presents the hazard of scratching the surface of the glass itself. Try to remove dirt on the glass by blowing it away or brushing with a camel-hair brush of the type used by photographers. For smudges, elevate the instrument and breathe upward on it (avoid getting saliva on the lens surface, as it may contain enzymes harmful to the coating). Then gently wipe the glass surface in a circular motion, using a piece of chamois, soft cloth, or optical tissue. If the smudge is persistent, moisten a soft cloth with a commercial lens-cleaning preparation or with medicinal alcohol and rub the lens surface gently. Dust and grit elsewhere on the instrument can be removed with a brush or with a blow of air. An ideal brush for this purpose is the type found on ordinary typewriter erasers. "Canned air" used by photographers to remove dust from photographic equipment provides a clean, convenient source of pressurized air for removing dust and grit from hard-to-reach crevices as well as from lens surfaces. Binoculars may be placed inside plastic bags for protection against water and dirt.

3. Treat 'em gently. Binoculars and telescopes are precision instruments. They contain numbers of elements which must be kept in perfect alignment in order to function properly. Don't bang or jar them. All binoculars and scopes, no matter what they cost, are breakable. The difference is that some are more breakable than others.

4. Use 'em in the shade. Direct sunlight falling on either the objective or ocular lens of binoculars or scopes creates flare and destroys image quality. Work with the sun at your back, if pos-

sible. If you cannot, contrive to cast a shadow on the lenses. Use the shadow of a tree, automobile, another observer, your hat, even your free hand to shade the lenses.

5. Never look at the sun or into strong light. Binoculars and telescopes collect a large beam of light and focus it into a small beam of greatly increased intensity. Looking at the sun, into glare on water, or at some other strong light source may produce permanent damage to the eyes by burning the cells in the fovea. The exception: Some telescopes and binoculars may be fitted with solar-observation filters that remove upward of 99.99 percent of the light. If you wish to observe the sun, make sure you use such a filter. Do not use exposed photographic film or some other inadequate substitute.

DEALERS AND REPAIR SERVICES

Many people prefer conducting business with a local dealer, which is fine. For those interested in dealerships that specialize in binoculars and scopes:

Discount sales: Birding, P.O. Box 5, Amsterdam, N.Y. 12010. A reputable, long-established mail-order discount house with discount prices on a wide range of brand-name telescopes and binoculars, all sold with manufacturers' guarantees. Birding does not offer a trial period, nor does it offer repair services. In my dealings with them the service has been exceptionally prompt, efficient, and courteous. Price lists upon request.

Retail sales: Mirakel Optical Co., Inc., 331 Mansion St., West Coxsackie, N.Y. 12192. Also a reputable, long-established firm which both sells and services a wide range of brand-name binoculars and telescopes. Prices are usually manufacturer's suggested retail, but Mirakel offers a thirty-day trial period and, in addition to the manufacturer's warranty, their own house warranty on items they sell. They also market a line of binoculars under their own brand name, made in Japan but "tuned up" in the Mirakel repair shop. Mirakel offers complete repair services and a number of modifications to improve the convenience of binoculars and scopes. Price lists upon request.

Questar telescopes: Questar, New Hope, Pa. 18938. Exclusive sales and services for Questar telescopes and a range of specialized accessories. Descriptive literature and price lists upon request. The Questar company welcomes prospective buyers to their plant and will give demonstrations of their products under field conditions. Though I have not visited their facilities, I have been told by friends that their visits were both enjoyable and informative.

VI

CONDITIONING

Success in seeking out wildlife is heavily dependent upon the proper functioning of one's muscles, senses, and mental awareness. Undoubtedly the best way to condition all of these to function well is to spend several hours every day in the outdoors in pursuit of quarry. Ordinarily, the more time spent outdoors, the higher one's conditioning becomes. In practice, however, it is not always possible to spend time outdoors every day, and skills that were sharpened by constant use begin to grow dull. It is possible to keep them honed to a keen edge, however, by following a simple program designed to keep the body and senses in good condition for outdoor activities.

Maintaining a keen condition is greatly helped if one follows sound health practices. The most important health habits were recently identified by the California Health Department's Human Population Laboratory after completion of a twenty-year study of 7,000 human subjects. In summary, the study cited seven basic health habits: (1) eating regularly, and not between meals; (2) eating breakfast; (3) keeping a normal weight, neither underweight nor overweight; (4) getting eight hours of sleep a night; (5) not smoking; (6) drinking moderately, not more than one or two alcoholic beverages a day; (7) exercising regularly. One of the authors of the study said, "A man at age fifty-five who follows all seven good health habits has the same physical health status as a person twenty-five to thirty years younger who follows less than two of the health practices." Obviously, good health benefits one in all areas of life, not just in enjoyment of the outdoors.

PHYSICAL CONDITIONING

The casual observer who limits himself to short, easy walks does not need a physical-fitness program. However, he may find that improving his physical condition also improves his sense of well-being, increases his self-esteem, and allows him to find greater enjoyment in all areas of life. He may find that as his strength and stamina increase, he gains the confidence and desire to go farther afield and thus improves the quantity and quality of his wildlife observations.

The person whose goals include intermediate to advanced activities will need increasing levels of physical fitness and, particularly if he leads an otherwise sedentary life, he will undoubtedly benefit from some kind of physical-conditioning program. Stalking through dense woods requires a good deal of

The advanced stalker is often required to move at a rapid pace over considerable stretches of difficult terrain while carrying heavy equipment. Good physical condition is necessary for such efforts.

bending and twisting to avoid the sound of limbs breaking or whistling across clothing; of stretching and balancing to step across logs, fallen limbs, ditches, and viny entanglements; and of stamina in order to freeze for prolonged periods, often in very uncomfortable positions. Hunters must often carry heavy game out through difficult terrain, and photographers sometimes pack cumbersome equipment over long distances. Perhaps the most demanding effort is the attempt to circle undetected around a concealing landform in order to intercept a quarry moving along a trail or path: The stalker must move quietly but rapidly, usually at a near-jogging pace, through pathless and often treacherous terrain, carrying one or more pieces of fairly heavy equipment. Unless the individual is in excellent physical shape he is very likely to pull a muscle, fall and break a bone, or even suffer a cardiac arrest. Advanced stalking frequently requires a high level of physical fitness that can only be attained by regular, rigorous exercise.

The primary physical requisites for successful advanced stalking are stamina, suppleness, coordination, and balance. Almost any physical exercise that improves these can be used as part of a conditioning program. Heavy weightlifting designed to build great muscle strength and bulk is about the only common form of exercise that does not yield good results for our purposes. I believe a nearly ideal conditioning program consists of a combination of walking, jogging, and calisthenics.

Walking is an excellent conditioning activity that promotes muscle tone throughout the body and also produces benefits to the respiratory, circulatory, digestive, and nervous systems. In addition, long, regular walks also build stamina. For maximum benefits a walking program should be followed every day that weather permits. Ideally, your conditioning walks should be over terrain similar to that where you plan to seek wild quarry. The rougher the terrain and the denser the vegetation, the better, for this will give you more vigorous workouts and will make the area where you do your actual stalking seem easy by comparison. These walks are a good time to break in footwear and other gear and to become accustomed to the weight of any equipment that will be carried in actual stalking. A gun, camera, or pair of binoculars that felt featherweight when first picked up comes to feel like a hunk of lead after being carried for a couple of hours by a person unaccustomed to the weight.

Many people, myself included, like to combine a walking routine with a program of jogging.

Jogging has become one of the most popular fitness exercises and its value is widely recognized. There are significant benefits to the circulatory, respiratory, and muscular systems, and many people feel that jogging reduces tension and promotes overall physical and emotional well-being. It is a nearly ideal method of building stamina and is a useful part of many weight-control programs.

If you are not in good physical condition but want to start jogging, ask your physician what kind of program he would recommend for you to start with. He may want to make a cardiogram before giving advice. Remember that attaining fitness requires time, despite the spurious claims of some so-called "twelve-day" fitness programs. The actual time will vary with your level of fitness when you start. For a person with normal health but little muscle tone, about six to eight weeks of daily exercise are required.

Start slowly, making small increases in the distances jogged each day. Do not attempt to do it all at once—a half-mile jogged six days a week will give beneficial results, whereas three miles jogged once a week probably will do more harm than good. At first you may expect some soreness and stiff muscles, but these symptoms should go away within a week. If they persist, you're doing too much and are overtaxing your muscles. Take three days off and start over, setting more moderate goals. During the building-up stage of your jogging program you should run at least five days a week. After you reach the goal you set of running a specific distance within a certain time, you can maintain that level of fitness by running three *nonconsecutive* days a week. However, if jogging is part of a weight-reducing program, it may yield better results if practiced every day.

How far and fast should you jog, once you've built yourself up to a satisfactory fitness level? That's entirely up to you, though it's probably true that the minimum distance should be at least one mile. Anything less than that will not yield very many benefits to a normally healthy adult. Those seeking great endurance will of course gradually build up to daily jogs of several miles and may bring their time down to near six-minute miles, or even lower. I've found that I feel satisfactorily fit when I routinely jog three miles a day, keeping my time somewhere between seven and seven and a half minutes per mile. If I have the opportunity to play tennis or some similar sport, I reduce the distance to a mile or a mile and a half. If I miss jogging more than two consecutive days I begin to feel restless and stale, but jogging again invariably leaves me feeling invigorated and refreshed.

Calisthenics provide a means of strengthening muscles and at the same time increasing suppleness, balance, and coordination. A good set of calisthenics will stretch and flex all major body muscle groups but, if performed correctly, will do so without risk of tearing or straining muscles. Calisthenics provide an excellent way of warming up before any physical effort, and I like to perform a set before jogging—I seem to run better and feel better at the end. I don't think it makes a great deal of difference what specific calisthenic movements are involved as long as each major muscle group is exercised. The standard movements used by physical-education classes, athletic teams, and armed forces personnel are all good. Anyone who is unfamiliar with these can find numerous descriptions in the physical-education sections of public libraries.

By toning up the muscles of the trunk and limbs and increasing overall body flexibility and balance, calisthenics condition an observer to move through the environment with greater stealth and sureness. A stalker moving through difficult terrain in many ways resembles a ballet dancer moving in slow motion. Frequently balancing on one foot, he follows a circuitous path, twisting and turning to step over, bend below, or swivel-hip around obstacles, often holding one or more limbs at extreme extension. It is interesting to note that ballet imposes tremendous physical demands on the performer. Doctors at the Institute of Sports Medicine and Training at the Lenox Hill Hospital in New York City recently made a study of the physical demands of various activities. They examined ten categories: strength, endurance, body type, flexibility, coordination, speed, agility, balance, intelligence, and creativity. When the results were totaled, ballet emerged as the most demanding activity—more demanding than basketball, soccer, football, or baseball. In stalking, as in other sports and physical arts, the greatest performances are made by those in superb physical condition.

SENSORY CONDITIONING

Good vision and hearing are of course extremely important to finding wildlife. Some people appear to have a natural facility for picking up the right sights and sounds; others who have not developed the proper techniques often have great difficulty and sometimes develop an attitude of "Some people can do this, but I can't." Usually such people will resist the idea that they could improve their visual and hearing abilities through learning and will argue that these abilities are "inborn." It is both gratifying and amusing to start a person of the "inborn" school of thought on some simple perception exercises and watch him a week or so later when he suddenly discovers that he can use his eyes and ears outdoors far better than the average person can. This discovery is almost always accompanied by surprise and an element of disbelief, for in the course of doing the exercises most people are unaware of their progress until they come up against another person whose perceptual skills are still undeveloped. Frequently you will hear your student say to his unlearned friend, "You mean you didn't hear and see that? You must be deaf and blind!" It's at this point that you can usually convert your student to support a theory of perceptual learning.

Among students of perceptual skills there are a diversity of learning rates; some make much more rapid progress than others. Also, individuals may acquire different skills at varying rates—one individual may progress rapidly in developing visual skills and slowly in hearing skills, while another student may reverse these rates. Most people can develop good proficiency in both areas even if they possess a handicap such as colorblindness or tone deafness. A person with normal vision (including corrected vision) and normal hearing can become quite expert in both. The elderly often lose the ability to hear high-pitched sounds such as bird songs in the extreme upper registers; this loss is so prevalent that many consider it normal, and though it does eliminate one's ability to hear certain frequencies of sound, the blocked-out portion of the sound spectrum is very narrow and the individual usually continues to hear other frequencies with normal sensitivity.

Let's consider the reasons why some people must learn to use their eyes in a new way in order to detect and identify birds and mammals in the wild. In another chapter we refer to two people, one of whom easily detected a small bird in the treetops and correctly identified it while the other saw the bird only after it had been pointed out and even then was unable to see the identifying marks. The successful observer used two visual techniques not used by the other. First, he scanned large portions of the environment by paying attention to the entire retinal image; second, he picked out fine detail by shifting attention to the sharpest portion of the retinal image, which is located in the small central area of greatest sensitivity, the fovea.

If these techniques are successful, why did the second observer not use them also? One answer, of course, could be that he simply was not trying. But more likely answers could be either that he was unaware of the techniques or that he had not practiced them enough to become proficient. It should be emphasized that neither technique is unnatural or harmful; it's just that our modern life-style predisposes us to develop different visual habits. Consider that for most of us the majority of our visual efforts are directed to rapid-scan reading at very close distances, or to looking at people, objects, or television at medium distances. There is little requirement to look at fine details and almost none to scan large portions of the environment. We develop habits of focusing at medium distances and on a portion of the visual field that is neither very large nor very small, because these are the habits that work very well in our urbanized life-style.

But when we go out into a large area of true wilderness we confront a different kind of visual field and the old habits are no longer the best ones. The visual field is much more complex and variegated; the distances to be covered, both in width and depth, are many times greater; and the critical features we are looking for are often perceived as very small images because either the animal itself is small, or it is seen at a great distance, or it is mostly concealed, or perhaps some combination of these factors. Any wildlife enthusiast can increase his success in finding and identifying quarry by practicing the two kinds of visual techniques until he can use them almost automatically, without conscious effort. Some simple exercises can help anyone learn these techniques.

Exercises for vision

These exercises do not improve your vision in the sense that they cause physical improvements in your eyes. In fact, they probably do not change them at all. What these exercises do is train you to *use* your eyes in new ways, and in fact I think they are really exercises in mental control—they encourage you to focus attention on areas of your retinal images that usually receive less than full attention. You may feel that you are "opening up" or "closing down" your visual images as you do the exercises, but actually you are not; the retinal image remains the same and you are only enlarging or constricting the scope of attention you direct to that image.

When you do the exercises with full concentration you may notice that your mind appears to move to an altered state of consciousness. What usually happens is that verbal thought patterns cease as consciousness devotes itself completely to perceiving the visual data pouring in from the eyes. This nonverbal state of consciousness is unsettling to some people at first, for they may fear that they are experiencing autohypnosis or are putting themselves in a trance. Actually it is a normal state of consciousness whenever we concentrate fully on any of the body senses—taste or sound or smell or touch or sight. Once the nonverbal state becomes familiar, it in fact becomes quite relaxing—moving into it seems to reawaken awareness of the body-self and reduce physical and emotional tension.

Here are some basic exercises. You may wish to invent variations of your own that are designed to achieve the same ends. It is best to practice them outdoors where focusing distances can be greatly varied, but this is not essential.

To develop peripheral vision that will enable you to scan large portions of the environment at once:

Sit comfortably, with head and eyes directed straight ahead.

Bring your hands together, palms inward, like the pages of a book at your normal reading distance directly in front of your face. Look at your little fingers, which should be touching. Look at the creases and folds and tiny wrinkles in the skin. Really look. Try to see very fine details.

Now part your hands and, moving your arms at the shoulders, bring your hands back toward the sides of your head. At the same time the focus-point of your eyes should shift to the medium distance, remaining straight ahead.

Now, without moving your eyes, try to see your hands. Move your hands forward or back until you can just begin to see them. Make fists and then hold up varying numbers of fingers from each hand. Visually count the fingers.

Now move your hands straight up and down, keeping your eyes fixed straight ahead. Notice how the images of your hands change. Now hold your hands still, level with your eyes, and direct your eyes first up, then down, repeating several times. Again notice how the images of your hands change.

Put your hands down and look straight ahead, fixing your eyes on some object in the medium distance. Without moving your eyes, begin directing your attention to other objects at varying distances and directions from the center of your visual field. See how far you can direct attention away from this center.

Close your eyes and rest them for a moment. Then fix them again on some object in the middle distance. Without moving your eyes, try to direct your attention away from the center of your visual field and make it sweep around the center like the movement of the second hand on a clock going at about three times normal speed. Go completely around once; then reverse and go around in the opposite direction. You may require two or three practice sessions to get the hang of this. Rest your eyes for one minute.

Now look at a fixed point in the middle distance and try to take in as much of your visual field as you can. Look for any movements you can detect anywhere in your field of view, but do not shift your eyes. Use all the peripheral vision you can muster. Try to identify each movement, using any visual clues you can—size, color, shape, type of motion, etc. Is it a leaf flicking in the breeze? A bird flying overhead? A small creature moving in the grass? An insect in flight? Practice this as long as you want and are comfortable with it. Try to practice briefly at the beginning of each outing in search for quarry.

To develop concentrated vision that will enable you to focus on very fine details:

Sit comfortably. Bring one hand up to your normal reading distance and begin to examine the back of your hand and wrist. Slowly flex the wrist and fingers. Notice the tiny lines and ridges in the skin. Look for very fine details.

Look at the skin over your forearm. Notice the small, sometimes subtle shifts in color from one spot to another.

Look at the hair growing on the back of your hand and wrist. Notice that individual hairs vary in size and shape. Look for the smallest one you can find. Examine it closely from root to tip, letting your eyes focus along its entire length. Try to examine the extreme tip.

Drop your hand and look at a plant a few feet away. Without

moving to it, pick out a leaf and look at its details. Notice the stem, the shape of the leaf; let your eyes work along the veins and wrinkles. Look for the finest details you can see.

Pick out several leaves on the plant and examine each one closely. Look for differences between the leaves. Examine the plant's stem or trunk, looking at surface details. If you can locate an insect moving on the plant, follow its movements closely.

Now shift to a plant in the medium distance. Pick out the tiniest details you can see. Look at an individual leaf, its stem, its edges and veins. Look for differences in color among various leaves.

Now shift to a subject in the far distance. Again, examine it closely for the finest details you can see.

If you use binoculars or a scope, repeat the exercises for medium and far distances using these items. Work for critical focusing of the mechanism, and if you begin to experience eyestrain, stop and rest. You should experience eyestrain only if the equipment is not properly adjusted or if it is deficient in optical quality. If strain does occur it will not cause damage or injury to the eyes, but will create eye discomfort and possibly headaches. After practicing with your binoculars or scope, practice again with your unaided eyes.

Continue these exercises for as long as you want and are comfortable. Try to practice briefly at the beginning of each trip in search of quarry.

Exercises for hearing

Hearing, like vision, can be controlled by mental attention so that it takes in a wide sweep of sound or focuses on one particular sound. Scientists often refer to this as the "cocktail-party phenomenon" because a room full of people grouped in conversational clusters provides a perfect illustration. A person can enter such a room and listen to the general hubbub of conversation without focusing on any one. He can then scan the room, listening for a particular topic of conversation, or perhaps a particular quality of voice, that interests him. When he finds it, he can then pay attention to that conversation exclusively, even though other conversations may be closer or louder than the one he is listening to. Just how we are able to pick out one sound from a matrix of competing sounds and listen exclusively to it is still something of a puzzle to scientists.

We can use our hearing in much the same way to search for wildlife. Upon entering an area, we can listen to the entire range of natural sounds, scanning for one that is of particular interest. When we detect such a sound we can focus our attention upon it almost exclusively.

To hear with complete success we must be able to do two things: to discriminate between similar sounds, and to correctly identify the producer of the sound. To the beginner the problem seems more complicated than it really is because the sounds of nature appear "different" and together may sound like an indistinguishable jumble. Indeed they are different to the person who has spent most of his life paying attention to the sounds of human voices, music, and machinery. The sounds of nature are often pitched in different frequencies and have markedly different coloration; but these differences do not make them more difficult to perceive correctly. In fact, once a person becomes familiar with them past a certain threshold, the "different" qualities of the individual sounds makes them all the more easy to identify.

The key to learning to discriminate between natural sounds is, again, practice. An excellent and very efficient way to gain practice is by listening to commercially available recordings of nature sounds (see the bibliography at the end of this book). Records are available of birds, frogs, insects, and other natural sounds. I recommend bird songs for reasons which will be stated later. By listening repeatedly and attentively to one of these recordings a person can gain a great deal of experience in a short time. The beginner will find that at first many of the songs sound so similar as to be indistinguishable one from another; but with repeated listenings he soon learns to discriminate between them and finally they begin to appear so different that he wonders how he could ever have confused them in the first place. He is learning to discriminate details, and this ability will carry over into other kinds of natural sounds as well. Thus the individual is learning not just bird songs, but the fine art of discriminating among an enormous range of natural sounds.

The next step is learning to identify the source of a sound. A common way of doing this involves learning to associate it with a visual image. This is facilitated in some bird-song recordings by the sounds being indexed to illustrations or discussions printed separately in a book. All the listener has to do is flip the pages to find a description or illustration of the bird producing the sound. Making this association is easy for a few people, but most require repeated practice sessions to gain proficiency. Modern field guides to birds also contain sonograms —chartlike visual representation of bird songs produced by electronic analysis of the songs. The person who can learn to "read" sonograms will find them extremely useful in field work.

But though recordings are useful, practice in the field is indispensable. Again, birds are a good place to start because they are abundant and vocal, and many different species are available for study. Extremely valuable experience can be gained through a knowledgeable friend who can identify bird songs and calls for you even if the bird is not visible, which is frequently the case. If you are working alone, the best procedure is to be an opportunist, taking advantage of the chance to learn the song or call of whatever birds you may encounter. A good method is to find and visually identify a bird and then study it for a while, through binoculars if possible. Notice its form, its color, and above all its movements as it produces a song or call. Then shut your eyes and listen for the sound again. Try to visualize in your mind's eye the bird's image and activity as it produces the sound. Usually only a few minutes spent with one species of bird will enable you to call up its mental image whenever you hear it again, and soon you will be identifying scores of species of birds by voice alone.

This same procedure may be used, of course, for sounds other than vocal ones. It is an easy way to learn to identify both birds and mammals moving about or foraging for food. If you watch the animal closely (making sure you identify it correctly) and then shut your eyes and mentally picture its activities as you listen to its sounds, you will soon be able to identify the species by sound with very high accuracy. After some experience you will be able to perform marvelously complex analyses of sounds that would put even a modern computer to shame. You will hear the sound of a creature moving on the forest floor and by analyzing volume and rhythm you will know almost immediately the creature's approximate size and weight, whether it is running, hopping, or walking, and the length of its stride. In an instant an image of the probable source will come to mind. You will know it as surely as you would recognize the footsteps of a member of your family in another room. And that is a very nice piece of work.

Birding as practice. Throughout this discussion I've made reference to birds, and for a reason. I'm not alone in recommending that anyone who wants to improve his skill in detecting and identifying wild creatures, either by vision or by sound, will find birding an ideal way of practicing. Birding can be done almost anywhere, even in most cities, and is a year-round pursuit. It costs practically nothing, provides a great deal of pleasure, and, when one feels ready to pursue the "difficult" species, he will be called upon to make extremely fine discriminations among details of appearance, voice, and behavior. At any level of difficulty, however, birding provides ideal practice in using one's eyes and ears outdoors and is a valuable hobby for the hunter or naturalist no matter what his particular specialty might be.

PSYCHOLOGICAL CONDITIONING

The mind is most aware of the natural world when it is completely receptive to the data being fed in through the senses. To achieve this it must be free from worry, distraction, or irrelevant thoughts. My experience with a number of observers suggests two main reasons why an individual may fail to give complete attention to the natural world around him: he may be distracted by worries over practical, workaday matters; or he may feel threatened by imaginary dangers in the wild. In the discussion immediately following we will look at some measures for freeing the mind of everyday concerns. The subject of dangers in the outdoors is sufficiently complex that it will be treated in a separate chapter.

Worry over practical matters is natural when we have been deeply involved in some problem, especially if for some time. During a long session of hard mental effort our bodies tense up and our minds get "grooved" into thinking constantly about the problem at hand; we tend to ignore the sights and sounds around us and in fact may consider them "distractions." In such a state of mind, it is possible to walk into the quiet solitude of a woodland and be so absorbed in thinking about our difficulties that we completely ignore our surroundings, and the myriad realities in the natural world are noticed only in bits and snatches, if at all. The best way I know to learn (or relearn) to be truly perceptive in the outdoors is to spend several days, alone, in solitary communion with nature. Gradually the body relaxes, the racing thoughts give way to repose, the repose to alertness, and the alertness to keen sensory perceptions. Then the mind has uncluttered itself and has attained to a Zen-like state that is at once alert yet peaceful, perceptive yet still. The experience has a calming, soothing effect that most people consider an antidote to the cares and frustrations of the workaday world, and, indeed, relaxing the body and renewing the senses is exactly what vacations are all about.

But spending several hours each day in contact with nature is not always possible. Even so, it helps to spend a few minutes each day trying to cultivate a calm psychological state. It seems to me that the longer one is away from mental repose, the more difficult it is to reacquire, and when I'm locked into a work routine I find it helpful to stop every few hours and look out the window at some natural scene and try to put myself as closely in contact with it as I can. This is not only a means of practicing the right psychological conditioning for wildlife observation; it is also a way of relaxing and improves my efficiency when I return to work.

There is another type of exercise I believe helpful in this regard, for it relaxes the body, clears the mind, and probably to some extent frees up the senses. It is described in detail by Dr. Herbert Benson of Harvard Medical School in his book *The Relaxation Response.* Basically the exercise consists in sitting comfortably in a quiet place, eyes closed, and breathing deeply and slowly while mentally repeating a word (Dr. Benson recommends the word "one") in rhythm with breathing. The goal is complete physical relaxation and an emptying of the mind of conscious thought. Anyone interested in the details of this type of exercise should refer to Dr. Benson's book. I am not a regular practitioner of this type of meditation exercise, but I have used it and believe it is an excellent way to make the transition from the world of work and worry into the green solitude of nature.

Equally valuable, in my judgment, is the practice of Hatha Yoga. I have experimented with this for several months and believe it to be an almost ideal relaxation technique for our purposes, for not only does it induce mental and emotional calm, it also benefits the physical system in a number of ways, among them improved flexibility, coordination, and balance. I strongly recommend it, particularly for those who during the ordinary work day frequently feel stressed or harried.

VII

ARE THERE DANGERS IN THE WILD?

Many people fear that "something" will happen to them in the wild. So caught up are they in their fears that they cannot devote proper attention to seeing and appreciating the natural world around them. This is a condition most likely to occur in people who are unfamiliar with wilderness, though it can occur in moderately seasoned observers who find themselves for the first time in a strange or unaccustomed environment. The fear takes many forms, and only occasionally is it based on realities. Some people are afraid of snakes; others of insects; still others of wild cats, bears, quicksand, lightning, flash floods, hidden crevices, solitude, and even armed bandits. Some city-bred people who are out in the wild for the first time find it extremely difficult to deal with these fears.

The experienced outdoorsman may be inclined to laugh at such people, but it must be remembered that the fears are quite real to those experiencing them. Proof of this is found in the records of those who by some misfortune were left alone in the wilderness, were seized by a terrifying panic, and by completely irrational behavior subjected themselves to exhaustion, injury, exposure, and perhaps death. Newcomers to unfamiliar wilderness areas, especially children, should never be left out of voice range of an experienced companion. And when they show signs of being afraid, they do not need ridicule, they need information.

The old saying that "the truth shall make you free" is very appropriate in learning to overcome fear of the outdoors. There is no question that the responsibility for most injuries and accidents in the wild rests clearly with the victim himself for acting with poor or uninformed judgment. A small number of dangers do exist out there, but all can be circumvented by proper action. The person who knows exactly what the dangers are and knows how to deal with them is called a good outdoorsman. Foolishly brave people who don't know what they are or how to deal with them are frequently called victims. Uninformed people who don't know what they are and are afraid of everything are called fraidy-cats.

A certain kind of folklore has it that hidden out there in our North American wilds are malicious, demonlike creatures just waiting to attack human victims. This is utter nonsense. The fact is that almost no animal in North America will attack a human being unless provoked, and danger from living creatures is virtually nonexistent to the person who handles himself properly. Of the thousands of species on the continent north of Mexico, only three species are regarded as aggressive toward man, and it should be emphasized that only a *percentage* of these three species are in fact aggressive. Moreover, the dangerous species are restricted in range, in numbers, or in both.

The only normally aggressive mammal in North America is the grizzly bear. Grizzlies are restricted to the Rocky Mountain states, western Canadian provinces, and Alaska. They do not "hunt" humans, but neither do they flee from them, and a few appear actually to resent human intrusion into their territories. Capable of great speed over short distances, they are enormously powerful and dangerous adversaries. Fortunately, they do not wander outside their narrow ranges and anyone elsewhere on the continent need have no fear of them.

The only other normally aggressive animals on our part of the continent are rare individuals of two species of reptiles. From the arid Southwestern states come vague reports of an occasional diamondback rattler that is "pugnacious"—just how much actual aggression must be displayed to earn this epithet is unspecified. The other species is the cottonmouth moccasin, found in the swamps and waterways of the Southeastern states. My friend Shirley Whitt is a trained herpetologist and has collected about a hundred of this species for study. She reports that five individuals exhibited aggression and moved toward her without provocation; the rest simply tried to escape. Neither of these species of reptiles is common in areas where there is much human activity for the obvious reason that they are quickly exterminated. Most individuals of both species actively fear man and will attempt to avoid his presence, and, in rare cases where aggression does occur, a human would normally have little or no difficulty in quickly escaping by just making a short sprint away from the slower-moving reptile, or by immobilizing it with a weapon.

Since the rare aggressive reptile is easily escaped by a reasonably watchful person, the only truly dangerous creature in the contiguous forty-eight states, then, is the grizzly. Those who must enter its narrow range should be prepared for the fact that though the probabilities for encountering an aggressive individual are quite small, the possibility does exist. In such an eventuality, there are four lines of defense. The best is probably to escape, if that is possible—up a tree, into a vehicle, into the water, or by any other available means. The second would be to immobilize the bear with a well-placed shot; however, the firearm should be of very heavy caliber and deliver quite a few foot-pounds of energy, and only the most steely nerved marksman is likely to be capable of precision shooting at a charging grizzly. The third line of defense is to fend off the creature by brandishing a flaming torch, which is possible if you happen to be near a campfire, but pretty difficult to pull off at a moment's notice in other circumstances. The fourth line of defense is admittedly last-ditch: you lie in a fetal position on the ground, hugging your knees, and "play dead." You are likely to be mauled about and injured some, but the total passivity and submission of this behavior appears, in actual instances, to have neutralized the aggression of these bears. This line of defense is not foolproof and undoubtedly living through it would be a painful and terrifying experience; but the alternative is to face off against 800 pounds of snarling fury that is only going to get more ferocious if it meets resistance.

But unless you go into wilderness areas within the well-defined range of the grizzly, you are not going to encounter one. This leaves the great majority of this continent free of really serious danger—more territory than you could possibly explore in several lifetimes. Throughout this vast region the chance of a lethal encounter with living creatures is extremely remote. Here are the remaining, less serious dangers, by classes of living things.

Mammals

Except for the grizzly, mammals are afraid of you and will leave you alone except in special circumstances. Almost any mammal, from the tiniest shrew on up to a moose, will defend itself if it feels threatened or intimidated. Drive any wild mammal into a corner, or attempt to put your hands on it, and it will almost certainly defend itself; otherwise it probably will make as speedy an escape as possible, or at the worst make intimidating gestures and allow you to back away gracefully. An injured or trapped animal will almost invariably attack a person who attempts to handle it—naturally fearful of humans, it cannot recognize that you may have intentions of trying to help it. Large animals that have been wounded—deer, or mountain lions, for instance—are positively dangerous and should be approached with extreme caution.

Remember too that most mammals have a strong instinct to protect their young, and an adult may become quite aggressive if you approach its immature offspring. Keep well away from the young of the larger, well-armed mammals such as bears (any species), mountain lions, bobcats, wolves, and various members of the deer family.

There are reports that the males of many species—from rabbits to moose—sometimes become belligerent toward humans who intrude upon their breeding territories during the peak of courtship. Apparently the highly aroused male, jealously guarding its territory, only attempts to drive intruders away and will not pursue a human much beyond the boundaries of its territory. Whether such an animal, normally quite fearful of man, would actually attack, or only put up a bluff, is problematical. In any case, such incidents are rare; I have never known anyone who actually had such an experience.

Rabies is a minor threat, but usually the presence of rabies in local populations is well publicized. A rabid mammal is reputed to be recognizable by its crazed behavior—a dazed appearance and faltering movements which convey an impression that the animal is confused, bewildered, aimless, and in pain. Fortunately the occurrence or rabies is rare and an infected animal, weakened by the disease, is seldom able to inflict serious tissue damage to a human victim. It is the infection which it transmits that is dangerous. If you are bitten or scratched by a mammal you suspect is rabid, make every attempt to kill or capture it and turn it over to health authorities for observation or examination. If it proves to be rabid, you can be protected by immunizing shots. If you cannot kill or capture the animal, immediately discuss the incident carefully with your physician.

Note: Unless you have special knowledge and equipment, never handle bats. Folklore to the contrary, bats are normally harmless, do not get tangled in people's hair, and do not (in North America, anyway) live on blood. Most species live entirely on insects, a few on fruit. But bats appear to have a peculiar immunity to rabies and may be carriers of the disease though they seem to be little affected by it. Verified cases of rabid bats are rare; nevertheless, for prudence's sake, avoid direct contact with them.

It is ironic that a discussion of dangers from mammals should have to mention domestic animals, but, at least in my section of the country, they can be dangerous. Aside from the occasional vicious guard dog which may be found on property almost anywhere, many farms contain livestock that has no fear of man. Occasionally a bull, a horse, or a boar hog will "turn mean," as local parlance has it, and will charge at most humans entering the pasture or lot where it is confined. The dangers are most severe for small children. When I walk across a strange pasture, I make a point of staying reasonably close to a fence, which provides adequate protection. It is worth remembering that many livestock will come running to a human in anticipation of being fed, and are actually quite harmless. In some circumstances this situation can appear extremely ambiguous.

One final remark about mammals. In many parts of the continent, wild or feral dogs have formed roving packs that live by killing wild game or livestock. There are records of feral dog packs intimidating and even attacking humans, though given the probable number of such dogs, the incidence of attacks on humans seems almost infinitesimally small. The danger should not be ignored, however. If you know of feral dogs in your area, discuss the matter with the proper authorities and push to have them captured or exterminated.

Birds

Birds are almost completely wary of man except around an active nest. If a person approaches a nest containing eggs or young, some parents will conceal themselves at a distance; others will scold nearby; some will attempt to decoy the human away with a broken-wing act; and some will make dive-bombing flights at the intruder. I have had mockingbirds and brown thrashers brush my face with their wings, and my friend Jerry Via has had hair pulled from his head by the beaks of flying terns when he approached their nest colonies; but most birds are harmless because they lack weapons with which to inflict injury. The exceptions are the well-armed hawks and owls. The smaller species are usually fearful of man; the larger, fiercer species, however, frequently become aggressive around their nests and even in flight can stab with their talons. Danger to unprotected eyes can be quite great. The larger owls are particularly dangerous, especially in dim light or darkness, because their aerial approaches are utterly silent. Except at their nests, however, all North American

The great horned owl, like some other larger raptorial birds, should be considered dangerous in defense of its nest. Note the large, powerful feet and long, curved talons, typical of most large birds of prey.

birds are harmless in the wild unless they are captured or handled.

Note: There is absolutely no truth to the old folktale that eagles attack and carry off human babies.

Reptiles

Snakes are undoubtedly the most misunderstood class of animals on the continent, despite widespread efforts to publicize the harmless and beneficial natures of most species. North of Mexico in North America, only four types are venomous. Three of these—the cottonmouth, the copperhead, and the rattlesnake—are related and are called *pit vipers*; the "pits" are small depressions on either side of their heads between the eyes and nostrils. These pits are heat-sensing organs and enable the vipers to seek out warm-blooded prey in darkness. These snakes strike by opening their large jaws extremely wide and driving two fangs—one on either side of the upper jaw—into the victim. The fangs are hollow and inject a toxic venom in the same manner as a hypodermic needle. The fourth venomous type is the coral snake, found only in the Gulf States and a small desert area of the Southwest. The coral snake is usually small, seldom exceeding eighteen inches in length, and has a very small mouth and fangs—so small, in fact, that it can effectively bite an adult human only by seizing a finger or toe in its mouth and chewing in order to inject venom. It almost never bites humans unless it is touched or handled. The usual victims are small children. The coral snake is marked by transverse yellow, red, and black bands, and is frequently confused with harmless species marked with the same colors. In the coral, red and yellow bands lie side-by-side; in harmless species, red and yellow bands are separated by black. A useful mnemonic device to help remember the distinction is this couplet:

Red and black, friend of Jack;
Red and yellow, kill a fellow.

The only other poisonous reptile on the continent north of Mexico is an endangered species of lizard, the Gila monster of the Southwestern desert. Reaching a maximum length of two feet, it is characterized by a thick body, short legs, and a spectacular black and coral skin that appears beaded. The usual Gila is shy and retiring and actively seeks to escape from humans, though occasionally one may appear pugnacious. If teased or threatened, any can put on a hissing, snapping display and can become quite aggressive. Like the coral snake, the Gila has a small mouth and must chew in order to inject its venom, which comes from short fangs on the lower jaw. Natt N. Dodge, an authority on desert dwellers, says of this creature that "it would be very difficult for one to bite a human unless it were teased or handled or stepped upon by a barefooted child. Please do not kill or capture Gila monsters. These interesting lizards are a unique feature of native desert wildlife threatened with extinction."

There are no other venomous reptiles in our area. Now, let's turn to the question often asked by novice outdoorsmen, "Should I worry about snakes?" My preferred answer is, "No. Not if you handle yourself properly." There are several reasons for this. First, the vast majority of snakes possess neither fangs nor venom. Second, even if you encounter a poisonous snake, the overwhelming odds are that you will never be bitten unless you make a wrong move. Third, in the slim eventuality that you are bitten, remember that a single snake bite in and of itself is usually not fatal to a human adult in good health. For the person who is not aware of these facts, an encounter with any species of snake, harmful or not, is likely to induce terror; and if such a person is actually bitten, the extreme terror he might feel is probably more dangerous than the bite itself. Let's look at these situations more closely.

In most areas of the continent the nonpoisonous snakes far outnumber the poisonous varieties. In many areas there are no poisonous snakes at all, and of course throughout most of our area, reptiles, being cold-blooded, go underground into hibernation during the cold winter months. Within their geographical ranges and preferred habitats, the numbers of poisonous species will be in inverse proportion to the numbers of humans active in the area—that is, there will usually be no poisonous snakes in a well-used city park and only a small number on farmland; the greatest numbers will occur in remote wilderness areas. These are probabilities, not certainties, for snakes are mobile and can turn up anywhere, and many water-loving species frequently do turn up in strange places after floods. But in many areas it is possible to go out and observe wildlife without any concern whatsoever about encountering a poisonous snake.

The easiest way to educate yourself to the dangers of snakebite in your area is to read or inquire about the poisonous species found in your region. Do not ask just anyone you meet in the gas station, because uninformed people usually consider all snakes to be "moccasins." Seek a knowledgeable authority. Good sources include field guides and books on the reptiles of a given state or province; most public libraries will have these. You need not learn all the species you may encounter; you will need to learn to identify only the poisonous species, and in most regions the number will be zero, one, or two. Learn to make an absolutely positive identification, taking into account subspecies and normal variations in colors and patterns. Reinforce your identifying skills with visits to zoos or natural-history museums. Learn the species' food habits and preferred habitats. Soon you will begin to view even the poisonous serpent without terror, but with a new, detached objectivity. Snakes may even become objects of special interest, and you may find yourself someday walking right up to a harmless species and examining it with admiration, perhaps picking it up and handling it. Reaching this stage may take some time, however, and the interim may contain moments when the old terror returns. For example, almost any snake may become confused during a noisy commotion created by several people and, in its panic, behave erratically. A very usual course in such circumstances is for the creature to start moving rapidly toward someone. But this behavior is motivated by fright, not aggression. Again, many harmless species are capable of a convincing display of aggression and may even strike an adversary. Since they possess no fangs or venom, the strike is harmless unless it breaks the skin, in which case an antiseptic should be applied to prevent a local infection.

Sometimes large snakes can be quite impressive in their own defense. I remember once encountering a handsome six-foot black snake when I was taking a mother beagle and her three adolescent puppies for an outing. One of the young beagles, almost fully grown, began to bark at and threaten the snake, which drew up into a coil, hissed, and vibrated its tail against the dry leaves exactly as the rattler would do. It made a couple of feints at the puppy, which continued to bark and move in closer and closer. Finally, with blinding speed the black snake struck the puppy squarely between the eyes; the blow sounded like the strong rap of a human knuckle against the dog's head. The young dog was immediately cured; he let out a yelp and scrambled several feet away. It is better to remember that harmless snakes can do this than to nearly die of fright in the belief that you've been bitten by a newly discovered, previously uncataloged species of venomous snake.

It is also well to remember that poisonous species normally pose no threat even at close range. This was illustrated recently when my friend Dr. Gwynn Ramsey was hiking a portion of the Appalachian Trail with his son. They stopped to look out over a vista, and after a while Gwynn glanced down and noticed an uncoiled timber rattler only inches from his son's foot. He put his hand to the young man's shoulder and gave a quick shove, forcing him to step sideways out of danger. There had been a period of perhaps a minute during which the snake could have struck, but it did not. This was a typical reptilian response, and is far different from the aggressive responses imagined by fearful people. An interesting sidelight on this matter has been noted, however. When several people are walking single-file along a trail and step over a snake concealed by rocks or vegetation, the person most likely to get bitten is the second or third in line. Apparently the snake can tolerate one or two people stepping over it, but as the repetitions mount, it feels threatened and is aroused to protective action.

If you are going to be in an area that probably contains poisonous snakes, then exercise reasonable caution. Undoubtedly the best protective measure is to avoid accidental contact. By far the greatest percentage of bites occur on the legs below the knees and on the arms below the elbows. The bites occur because someone puts a hand or foot on or near a snake, touching it or frightening it and triggering an almost reflexive retaliatory response. This experience is easily avoided by the simplest of measures: Look before you place your feet or hands.

This doesn't mean that you must constantly be on the alert, looking everywhere, for snakes do not habituate open terrain. Like most wild creatures, they feel exposed and vulnerable in such conditions, and prefer to be near cover which provides an opportunity to escape from enemies. They like to be near a protective crevice or crevices such as might be provided by a log, hollow stump, rockpile, woodpile, creek bank, or whatever. If you examine places like these before putting a hand or foot there, chances are you will never be bitten. Leave the snake alone and it will leave you alone.

Despite all this, it is still possible, you say, to step on a snake accidentally and be bitten. Quite so. The chances are small, but still it does happen. But there are two forms of additional insurance. One is to carry a snakebite kit. The one I carry is made by Cutters and is available in most drug stores and outdoor-supply houses for about $3. About the size of a 35mm film roll, it fits easily into a pocket and consists of a cunningly designed set of rubber suction cups, a tourniquet, a sterilizing agent, a blade for making incisions, and complete set of instructions. I would advise anyone who is going to be exposed to possible bites to carry a snakebite kit, just in case, and to become thoroughly familiar with the instructions for its use. The second form of insurance is to wear protective boots. In my opinion this is necessary only in remote areas known to be infested with heavy concentrations of pit vipers.

If you should get bitten by a poisonous snake, remember that the most important thing to do is to remain rational and calm. You will probably feel a great surge of gut fear, for the prospect of dying is unsettling to almost anyone. Remember, however, that if you are a healthy adult, your chances of surviving even without medical attention are overwhelmingly good. Almost all deaths occur in children, adults in poor health, or in healthy adults who die from a combination of venom and panic, panic being the critical factor. Try to separate in your mind the effects of the bite and the effects of the fear you may be feeling. Fear causes an elevation in blood pressure, a noticeable increase in heart rate, labored breathing, and feelings of mental and physical restlessness. The effects are immediate, unlike those of a snakebite, which require some time to appear. Accept the fear as natural, do not be disturbed by the increase in your pulse and breathing rates, and recognize that you can assume complete control of the situation. Gradually your excitement and its symptoms will subside.

If possible, immediately kill the offending snake if you can do so within one minute or less. This will not only make you feel better; it is protection against a second bite (to you or someone else) and will allow you to make a careful, accurate identification of the species and the size of the snake, information that will be helpful to your physician in determining how to proceed with treatment. A snake can be easily immobilized by breaking its spine with a stick or rock. Then administer the *coup de grace* by pressing the snake's neck securely to the ground with a stick and crushing its head with a rock, boot heel, or anything else you find handy. After death the snake will coil and thrash about for some time and should be considered dangerous, for in its reflexive coiling it can still administer a strike. Pinion it down to prevent it from flopping away and disappearing.

Next, unless you can reach a physician within about an hour (half an hour for coral snakes), take first-aid precautions. Make simple, clean, shallow (¼ inch deep), longitudinal incisions over the fang wounds and draw out as much of the venom as possible, following the instructions provided in your snakebite kit. But be very careful. Some authorities advise against this procedure because many times in making incisions an excited and nervous victim cuts too deeply or cuts laterally through nerves, arteries, veins, muscles, or tendons. The wound may be worse than the snakebite. However, carefully made, correct incisions will enable you to draw out some of the venom. Then you must face two alternatives. One is to get medical attention as soon as possible, either by sending a companion for help or by seeking it yourself. The other is to stay put and tough it out, which is probably the best choice if you are in a remote area where an attempt to get out would require great exertion. Make yourself as comfortable as possible and prepare to spend about two days feeling sick. Do not take alcohol, depressants, or stimulants; do try to keep the area of the bite as cool as you can, probably by bathing it in the coldest water you can find. Move about as little as possible. You will probably vomit, feel feverish, have headaches, and generally feel pretty bad. An area around and above the bite will be very painful and will swell considerably, and any constricting clothing, rings, or bracelets near the bite should be removed immediately after the bite. After the ordeal is over you will be as good as new. If you are strong enough to be stomping around in remote wilderness areas, you are almost certainly strong enough to survive a snakebite.

One other North American reptile can be dangerous to humans. The alligator, found in the swamps and bayous of the Gulf States, is capable of inflicting severe damage with its enormous jaws and teeth, or even by lashing out with its powerful, muscular tail. Large alligators are sometimes quite bold and ferocious toward humans who approach them too closely. They are most dangerous in water, where their large tails make them powerful swimmers; on land their short legs make them slow and awkward. They pose no serious threat except in the waterways along the Gulf of Mexico.

Insects

Most people readily recognize stinging insects, predominantly wasps and bees. These insects are not aggressive unless they or their nests are threatened, in which case they can be vicious. The best policy is to stay clear of their nesting sites or hives, many of which are exposed to view and are easily recognizable, being globular or geometrical structures of a gray, paperlike material, sometimes of mud. Wasps often nest under the eaves of inhabited buildings and are especially fond of the interiors of abandoned or seldom-used buildings and sheds. Bees prefer hollow trees or the hollow walls of old buildings. Some wasps construct hives in tunnels beneath the ground, usually with a well-concealed entrance, and I know of no way to avoid stepping on the openings and triggering a flurry of attacks. Fortunately such underground hives are relatively rare. The best defense against aroused wasps or bees is simply to run like hell. You can avoid stepping on foraging individuals by being watchful when walking among flowers or among fruit that has fallen from trees.

The irritation from a bee sting is caused by venom injected from a tiny stinger located on the rear of the bee's body. A bee inserts the tiny barbed stinger beneath the skin, and ordinarily the stinger is torn from the bee's body when it escapes, along with the tiny venom sac. Consequently, if you are stung by a bee, do not grasp the stinger between your fingers to remove it; in doing so, you squeeze the venom sac and inject more venom. Remove the stinger by scraping it off with a fingernail, knife blade, or something similar. Prompt removal will significantly lessen the amount of venom which enters the wound. A number of ointments and sprays are available in most drug stores to reduce the pain of stings.

Wasp and bee stings, unless delivered in numbers, ordinarily cause only local pain and irritation. A few people, however, have allergic reactions to stings, and these can be quite serious if not given prompt medical treatment—in fact, each year in the United States more people die of bee stings than of snakebites. Allergic responses include welting of skin over the entire body, itching of skin on the palms of the hands and soles of the feet, headache, nausea and vomiting, a rash and swelling inside the throat, and weak and rapid heartbeat. A person exhibiting such responses should be kept quiet and taken to a physician or hospital as quickly as possible. In the meantime, antihistamines of the type used to treat common allergies may be given in normal dosages and may have some alleviating effects.

Persons who are allergic to stings need not give up outdoor activities if they keep a treatment kit close at hand during insect season. A kit is small and inexpensive and may be assembled on a prescription basis by a pharmacist, along with a complete set of instructions. Consult with your family physician for details.

On a less serious side, many insects, including the wormlike larval stages, can administer irritating stings and bites. These usually amount only to local irritation; allergic responses are rare, but show the same symptoms described above.

Bees possess a sense of smell, which they use to locate flowers, and they are apparently attracted by the flowerlike smell of a number of common after-shaves, perfumes, and colognes. Wear a nice insect repellent instead.

Spiders

Often confused with insects, spiders differ in having only two body regions (instead of three for insects), eight legs (instead of six), no antennae, and no wings, as well as in other respects. They are familiar creatures to most people, who readily identify them by their web-building habits. Almost all spiders are venomous and use their venom, which they inject by biting, to immobilize their insect prey. But only two species are considered harmful to man: the black widow, and the brown recluse.

The black widow has been found in all forty-eight contiguous states except Maine, where its existence is probable. According to my friend Dr. James Carico, an international authority on spiders, the black widow is such a shy and retiring creature that it will not bite even when its web is molested. It will bite, in fact, only if it is actually touched while in contact with the victim's skin. Danger is easily avoided by using care in the sites these spiders prefer for web-building. The web is almost never placed out in the open, but rather in a sheltered area, usually with overhead protection. Typical sites include the crawl space beneath houses; the eaves or interiors of sheds and outhouses; unused machinery; trash; rodent holes; hollow logs; and piles of lumber, wood, brush, or rock.

Members of the widow genus are fairly easy to recognize. They range in color from jet black to brownish black; the abdomen is large and globular, almost marble-shaped; the body appears shiny, as if lacking hairs. Throughout most of the United States, the widow has a red hourglass-shaped mark on the underside of its abdomen, though in some areas this may vary to form two triangles or spots. Only the female is dangerous. She is rarely found away from her web, which is coarse, irregular, and constructed of surprisingly strong silk. Ordinarily she is found hanging upside down in the web.

The bite of a widow is extremely painful and can be lethal. It is usually experienced as a pinprick sensation on the skin, and immediate investigation may show the spider still clinging to the body with its fangs inserted through the skin. The bite usually burns for a few minutes, followed by pain progressing up or down the bitten member. Gradually the pain tends to localize in the back or abdomen; abdominal cramps may become severe as the reaction progresses. The victim may also experience nausea, tremors, fever, and other discomforts. The height of the reaction may occur anywhere from a few minutes to a few hours after the bite. The reaction is normally self-limiting, and medical treatment consists of drugs to control pain and relax the muscles; large amounts of water should be taken, and some researchers have found massive doses of vitamin C (ascorbic acid) to be helpful. The victim should receive medical attention as soon as possible in order to reduce suffering. Recovery usually takes two or three days. Deaths do occur, but the mortality rate from bites by black widows is only about 1 percent and is usually limited to small children, the aged, or the infirm.

The brown recluse has a normal distribution bounded by a line drawn due north through central Texas to the northern border of Kansas, due east to the western border of Ohio, southeast to Atlanta, Georgia, and southwest through the western tip of Florida. Its habits predispose it to live in storage containers, and specimens have been found in isolation in widely dispersed locales, apparently having traveled in household goods shipped out of its normal range.

The brown recluse most frequently lives in cracks and crevices, spinning a highly irregular web near its shelter. In color it ranges from a light fawn to a chocolate brown. The body appears to be hairless unless viewed under magnification. The back is marked by a dark, fiddle-shaped design that is broad behind the eyes and narrows to a thin line near the middle of the back. This mark is distinctive and distinguishes the recluse from other common brown spiders.

The effects of a brown recluse bite differ markedly from those of a black widow. Pain may or may not be felt immediately after the bite; but in either case, the first symptom is a stinging sensation followed by severe pain. A blister usually rises over the wound, followed by pain and swelling in the general region, accompanied by nervousness, fever, nausea, and possibly pain in the joints. The tissue affected by the venom gradually dies and sloughs away, exposing the underlying muscle. The area affected may range in size from that of a penny to a half-dollar. Healing takes place slowly (up to eight weeks), but scar tissue gradually accumulates and forms a sunken scar. First-aid treatment consists of applying a local antiseptic to prevent infection, and the application of a cold pack to slow the effects of the venom. The victim should be placed in the care of a physician as soon as possible. Mortality from brown recluse bites is quite low and is usually restricted to children.

A few other species can inflict stinging bites, but no other spiders are truly dangerous to man, including the much maligned tarantulas of the Southwest. Tarantulas actually make pleasant pets, and, like all spiders, are beneficial in that they devour large numbers of noxious insects. With the exceptions of the widow and the brown recluse, spiders should not be wantonly killed, and many people condone their presence in suitable places.

Scorpions

Related to spiders, scorpions have large, pincerlike front legs and a long, slender tail equipped with a sting on the end. They are most abundant in regions with hot, dry climates, notably the Southwest. All species can sting, some painfully; only one species commonly found in the United States is deadly, and its greatest threat is to small children under four years of age. Multiple stings by this species, however, or single stings along the neck or spine, can be dangerous even to an adult. The dangerous species is about two inches in length, yellow or straw-colored, and markedly slender. Other species that occur with it are generally larger, darker, perhaps striped, and bulkier in appearance. The effect of a nondeadly species is local pain at the site of the sting only; the effects of the deadly species include local pain without swelling, and general responses over the entire body characterized by muscle contractions, especially in the abdomen, arms, and legs. There is usually a high fever, increased heart rate, and difficulty in breathing. Symptoms may resemble those of acute bronchial asthma. In the fatal cases observed, the affected children apparently died of exhaustion. First aid to the victim consists of applying cold packs to the wound to slow the effects of the venom. Prompt medical attention is imperative for adult victims with stings in vulnerable areas, and for children, the aged, and anyone in poor health.

Scorpions are active at night, and usually spend the daylight hours concealed beneath loose bark, rocks, and lumber. At night they may invade human dwellings if suitable entranceways exist. They may then conceal themselves in bedding or clothing, which should be examined prior to use. Scorpions are not found in most portions of the United States, but those intending to be active in the arid Southwest should familiarize themselves with the one deadly species, *Centruroides sculpturatis*.

Poisonous plants

Plants, like almost all living things, benefit from some form of self-protection to ward off enemies—in their case, primarily destructive birds, mammals, insects, and fungi. Many have developed thorns, stinging bristles, foul tastes or odors, or poisonous substances that discourage predation. A small number of plants concentrate sufficient amounts of poison in some parts of the plant to be deadly to humans who eat that part of the plant. Others contain enough toxins in some part of the plant to cause illness if eaten. Poisonous substances are found not only in wild plants, but in common domesticated plants as well. The potato, for instance, is a member of the deadly nightshade family and its leaves contain traces of a lethal poison; the foliage of many common garden flowers, including larkspur, clematis, lupine, and some lilies, contains poisons. These familiar domestic plants are not dangerous because the poisonous parts are seldom or never eaten. The same is true of many wild plants—they are not dangerous unless they are eaten, and there is no need to regard even the really poisonous ones as "dangerous" unless you go around chewing on them. The sole exceptions, perhaps, are mushrooms of the genus *Amanita*, some of which rank as extremely dangerous. One friend of mine who teaches natural-history courses during the summer insists that her students thoroughly wash their hands after handling *Amanita verna* to remove any traces of its toxins from their skin, so deadly is this mushroom whose common name is "destroying angel." Many species of mushrooms are poisonous in varying degrees. If you wish to collect wild mushrooms for the table, acquire a good field guide and study it carefully, and then be extremely critical in making your identifications in the field. Above all, do not depend on folklore such as "If a mushroom cap peels under the fingernail, it is edible," or "If wild animals eat the mushroom, it is safe for humans." Listening to folktales about mushrooms can lead to your being very sick or dead.

Several common North American plants can cause skin irritations if they are touched. The most common belong to the genus *Rhus*—poison oak, poison ivy, and poison sumac. All contain the same irritant, a heavy oil that produces an itchy rash on the skin of a person lacking immunity. Many people are immune and are unaffected, but immunity may be lost (or gained) at any time. No part of these plants should ever be eaten, even if you have immunity, nor should you come into contact with or breathe smoke from burning plants. Poison oak and poison ivy may be recognized by their three-parted leaves. A helpful saying is "Leaflets three, let it be." Poison oak is always an erect shrub; poison ivy may be an erect shrub, a trailing vine, or a climber. Poison sumac should not be confused with the harmless winged, staghorn, or smooth sumacs. It has seven to thirteen pointed leaflets *without teeth*, and produces *white* fruit. It is found almost exclusively in swampy environs.

Several other species of plants possess hairs, spines, or thorns that can cause local irritation or injury, but under ordinary circumstances none can be considered truly poisonous.

This concludes the catalog of living things that can ordinarily be considered "dangerous" in the wild. Actually, most of the dangers are likely to result in irritation, discomfort, or pain, not death. The only animal which might ordinarily be expected to attack and pose the threat of violent tissue damage is the grizzly. A healthy adult can usually survive the other dangers, though medical attention is desirable in the rare cases where danger to life does exist. But the rules of safe conduct to avoid serious danger are really very few, and certainly easy to follow:

1. Beware of the grizzly if you are in its range.

2. Keep out of the way of animals that are cornered or trapped, or that behave erratically; approach wounded animals with extreme caution.

3. Keep away from the young, dens, and nests of all large mammals and raptorial birds.

4. Do not put hands or feet in or near concealed places that may harbor poisonous snakes, insects, spiders, or scorpions.

5. If you're in an area where poisonous snakes are found, carry a snakebite kit; if poisonous species are abundant, wear thick, high-topped boots as an extra precaution.

6. If you encounter a dangerous situation, keep calm. Make a rational, common-sense choice of the safest way out, and chances are you will not be injured.

I hope this discussion will be some help to newcomers who may have heard exaggerated tales of how dangerous it is "out there." In over thirty years of spending a lot of time alone among the woods, fields, streams, and rivers as a child, adolescent, and adult, I have never had an experience that was injurious or even truly dangerous. I asked Dr. Ruskin Freer to comment on his experiences in this regard. At age eighty-four he is still active after having spent more than fifty years botanizing on thousands of acres of the Blue Ridge, often in remote and seldom-traveled territory. Here are his remarks:

Over the years I have encountered many rattlers and copperheads and without exception they were either making a rapid exit or were at least motionless and very apprehensive. They never attacked or threatened attack except in self-defense. I had several very intimate contacts with copperheads, when they were only inches away, or in three cases in actual contact with my shoes.

Several times we have sighted bobcats, always on the run, putting as much distance as possible between themselves and human intruders in their domain. Of course they will savagely defend themselves if cornered.

I have seen black bears only twice, but in each case they were wasting no time in leaving the scene.

*After numerous reports of mountain lions in our area in re-
cent years, not accepted by rangers of the National Park Service, Blue Ridge Parkway personnel finally themselves saw
and reported seeing mountain lions, but no hazardous situations have been reported and are certainly unlikely to happen.*

*While reasonable caution should always be practiced with
possibly dangerous forms of wildlife in our area, the assurance
that such creatures are either in flight or more apprehensive
than their human observers should be reassuring.*

Dangers from nonliving things

Probably the most common injuries in the outdoors result from
falls. A young girl goes racing along a forest path, trips on a tree
root, and breaks her arm in the fall. Or a man wants to photograph a waterfall, stands near the ledge, loses his footing on
the slippery rock, and plunges to the bottom. Was the tree limb
at fault? Was the rock to be blamed for being slippery? Certainly not. Most falls can be avoided by the most elementary
common sense: Walk, don't run; look before you step; don't
take chances. Youthful exuberance is one major cause of such
accidents; another is the vacant space in the heads of some
adults. Remember that one thing in nature never ceases operation, not even for an instant, and that thing is gravity. When
walking, work with it by maintaining your balance and
keeping a firm footing, always.

Gravity also extends above you and can pull objects down on
your head if you happen to be in the wrong place at the wrong
time. Dead tree limbs and even entire dead trees pose a threat
that can become serious during high winds or following an ice
or snow storm. In mountainous terrain, snow or rock can ava-
lanche downhill with devastating results. Many steep moun-
tainsides are marked by areas of scree—rock debris resulting
from a landslide. Frequently the scree is precariously balanced
and very little disturbance—such as a person walking across
it—can set the whole thing in motion again. Be cautious in
crossing slide areas and go around them if possible. It is a horri-
ble fate to be injured or killed by land erosion.

Lightning is a serious threat during electrical storms and
should be regarded with great respect. If you're caught outdoors
during such a storm, keep clear of tall objects that can act as
lightning rods—tall trees, or, in mountainous country, steep
inclines, shallow caves, and, worst of all, overhanging rock

ledges. Seek out the shelter of shorter trees and gentle slopes. If you're exposed in open country, remember that you may be the tallest object around and may act as your own lightning rod. Find a depression and crouch low, touching the ground only with your shoes. Try to keep dry, and if there is any way possible to do so, insulate yourself from the ground with a nonconductive material such as a rubber poncho.

Quicksand is so rare in the United States that it can be virtually ignored except in well-publicized areas. If you're uncertain, test the footing cautiously before putting your entire weight on it. If by some improbable chance you believe you've actually ventured onto quicksand, simply lie prone to distribute your weight over a large area and do a modified butterfly stroke to firm ground. You'll be perfectly safe this way.

Flash floods occur in very narrow, steep-sided gorges and arroyos, but only following heavy rains or cloudbursts. Heavy storms, tropical storms, and tornado conditions are now so well publicized in advance that no one should be surprised by such events unless he has been out of touch with civilization for several days. In that case, you should be watchful for storm-like conditions upstream and get out of low-lying areas when these conditions occur.

Extreme weather poses some hazards if you expose yourself without adequate preparation. In extremely cold conditions, if you're not properly dressed you run a risk of hypothermia, which means that your body loses heat faster than it can produce it and your body temperature may plummet, leaving you groggy, helpless, and probably in critical condition even if you receive help. There is also some danger from frostbite. At the other temperature extreme, in hot, desertlike conditions it is easy to suffer dehydration if your liquid intake is inadequate; dehydration can lead to a dangerous kind of stupefaction which is almost guaranteed to make you self-destruct. Another danger from hot climates is heat stroke. Again the solution to these problems is obvious: Don't expose yourself to extreme climatic conditions unless you are adequately prepared for them.

Obviously, there are some dangers in the wild, but a little reflection will show that every one of them can be rendered harmless by the use of simple common sense. If you exercise reasonable care, you're much safer in a natural area than you are driving down the freeway.

VIII

GETTING BIRDS AND MAMMALS TO COME TO YOU

Hunters, photographers, wildlife biologists, and the just plain curious often entice animals into a certain area by using bait, decoys, calls, or other lures. The results can be spectacularly successful, providing anything from a momentary glimpse of a shy, secretive animal to months-long observations and the possibilities of "making friends" with a particular creature. For ex-

Appropriate food placed in the right location will often attract large numbers of small birds and mammals, particularly in winter. Despite the photographer's presence behind a windowpane only inches away, this pert Carolina chickadee came readily to the free meal found in this window feeder.

ample, staking out a live rabbit near a wood margin may bring a large accipiter hawk, an owl, or a fox briefly into view. Planting a food patch near a woods or stream may bring daily (or nightly) visits from deer, raccoons, woodchucks, rabbits, and other herbivores for a whole season.

Baiting with food

The above examples illustrate the simple and common practice of baiting birds and mammals with food. To be effective, the bait must be placed inside, or at least very close to, the borders of the individual animal's territory. For most creatures the bait must also be placed close enough to protective cover so the animal will feel that it has a convenient escape route if it should have to flee. Very few animals will venture far into a completely open area where they would feel exposed.

The effectiveness of food in attracting an animal depends upon several factors. It must, of course, be situated so the quarry can easily find it—that is, it must be visible to a quarry that would locate it by sight, and upwind of a quarry that would locate it by smell. It should also look natural and, for most mammals, be free of human scent. Even if it meets these requirements it will attract a creature only if it is the right kind of food and the creature is hungry. For instance, a Cooper's hawk would not be attracted to cereal grains because it lives on a diet of flesh; but if it had recently eaten and had a full crop, neither would it be attracted to a staked-out pigeon or rabbit. It follows, then, that the best time to use food as bait is during a time when natural foods are most scarce, as in late winter. In other seasons there may be an abundance of vegetable matter, fruits, seeds, insects, and young animals to provide a readily available food supply for almost all creatures, birds and mammals, predators and prey alike. Under such circumstances, wild creatures are seldom very hungry and almost never desperately so, and consequently their naturally suspicious natures will cause them to shy away from bait, which, unless placed expertly, will appear somewhat unnatural. The exceptions are food plants, which attract herbivores during the planting or growing season. Many gardeners and farmers have found to their irritation that seeds and sprouts attract a number of birds and that young plants attract a number of different herbivorous mammals. But the wildlife enthusiast can, with planning, deliberately use the attracting powers of plants to his own advantage. Most state game commissions or universities can recommend specific plants for wildlife food in local areas.

In the late winter months, food is scarcer for most creatures, and particularly during hard weather animals are sometimes desperately hungry and will be attracted to bait that in other seasons they would probably ignore. It would obviously be impracticable to attempt to list all possible bait substances for birds and mammals. If you are interested in a particular species, reading a life history of the species will usually give you a fairly good idea of the creature's diet and foraging habits, and management literature will usually list proven baits.

Among the most common food baits are corn (whole and cracked) and other cereal grains, which attract a wide variety of birds and mammals; canned dog food, cat food, and fish products, which attract carnivorous mammals; and carrots, lettuce, apples, onions, and other vegetables, which attract rabbits and similar herbivores. Small mammals such as field mice, often baited in large numbers, may be attracted to the following mixture, taken from *Wildlife Management Techniques*, Robert H. Giles, editor (Washington, D.C.: The Wildlife Society, 1971).

2 lbs. melted beef suet
2 lbs. peanut butter
2 lbs. raisins, ground
2 lbs. oatmeal
1 lb. high melting-point paraffin

Other bait suggestions are published by Havahart Traps, Box 551, Ossining, N.Y. 10562. This firm sells a line of excellent box traps that catch animals alive without harming them in any way. Their recommended baits are described in *Trapping with Humane Havahart Traps*, and are quoted here with the company's permission:

ARMADILLOS: Mealworms, other worms, or insects enclosed in a little cloth bag; maggots, sardines, fish.

BIRDS: Undesirable birds as starlings, pigeons, etc., may be taken in Havahart No. 1 and 2 traps, one at a time, using such baits as sunflower seeds or scratch grain, run in one door and out the other. The birds follow the bait through the trap, tripping it when they hop on the bait pan. Starlings are especially fond of raisins.

CAT OR BOBCAT: Fish, meats, oil of catnip, sardines.

CHIPMUNK: Prune pits, unroasted peanuts, corn, sunflower seeds, peanut butter, cereal, grains, popcorn.

FLYING SQUIRREL: Apples, seeds, red rubber ball. (One of our exterminators told us he eliminated all the flying squirrels from a house using one of our traps and a red rubber ball for bait.) Whole roasted peanuts.

FOX, RED AND GRAY: Scented bait from reliable fox trapper, chicken, rabbit (in form of live bait). Provide live bait with comfortable quarters, food and water, then place trap so that the fox will pass through trap in trying to reach live bait.

GOPHERS: Peanut butter mixed with molasses, spread on whole wheat bread.

MICE: Cheese, bread and butter, small nuts, cherry pits, oatmeal, sunflower or similar seeds. Mixed peanut butter and oatmeal is very good bait, also gum drops, absorbent cotton, or flour. These baits are also good for rats.

MINK: Chicken head and entrails, fresh fish, fish-oil scent, part of rabbit, muskrat, red squirrel, mice, fresh liver.

MINNOWS: Stale bread, popcorn.

MUSKRAT: Fresh vegetables, parsnips, carrots, sweet apples, oil of anise, or musk from another muskrat.

NUTRIA: Muskmelon or cantaloupe rind, ripe bananas.

OPOSSUM: Vegetables, sweet apples, chicken entrails, sardines, crisp bacon, canned cat food.

OTTER: Fish.

PORCUPINE: Apples, salt, carrots.

RABBIT: Fresh vegetables such as brussels sprouts, cabbage, carrots, lettuce, or apples. In the wintertime, bread is a good bait. Vegetables have a lot of water in them, and in the cold weather they freeze stiff. Spraying the inside of the trap with apple cider has also proved effective.

RACCOON: Fish, fresh or canned, honey- or sugar-covered vegetables, smoked fish, watermelon, sweet corn, cooked fatty meat, crisp bacon.

RAT: Cheese, chicken or other fowl flesh, cereal grains, cracknels (cracknels, made from bacon scraps or other fatty meats, generally attract mink, weasel, skunks, rats and the like), peanut butter and oatmeal mixed, peppermint candy.

RINGTAIL OR CIVET CATS: Same as raccoon.

SKUNK: Chicken entrails, cracknels, fish—canned or fresh —insect larvae such as May beetles, crisp bacon.

SNAKE: Whole eggs (bantam), live mice.

SNAPPING TURTLE: Freshly chopped fish or freshly chopped chicken entrails. Put bait inside tin can in which numerous holes have been punched. Also any whole fresh fish pieces tied to trip wire.

SQUIRREL: Cereals, grains, nuts (especially peanuts, preferably unroasted), sunflower seeds, anise oil (a drop or two on bread). Mixed peanut butter and oatmeal or peanut butter and molasses is very good bait, also popcorn, milo.

WEASEL: Fish, fresh liver, chicken entrails.

WOODCHUCK: Fresh string beans, sweet corn, lettuce, peas.

VOLES: Peanut butter mixed with molasses, spread on whole wheat bread.

Some cautions: In using cereal grains for bait, make sure that the grain is untreated—that is, that it has not been treated in preparation for use in seed planting. Treatment chemicals can be highly toxic to wild animals. Flesh-eating predators are sometimes baited with small live birds or mammals commonly found in their diets. Wild mice and rats, rabbits, gophers, and small birds up to pigeon size have traditionally been used for both avian and mammalian predators. However, federal regulations now prohibit individuals from trapping or possessing many species of wild birds and mammals for any purposes, including use as live bait, unless specifically licensed to do so. If you are interested in this kind of activity, be sure to study the laws regarding possession of wild animals in your area before proceeding. You should also anticipate that staking out live bait requires great skill in order to avoid suffering and injury to either prey or predator. Baiting predators is a difficult art and should not be attempted by the novice.

Food is not the only physical allurement to birds and mammals. Once we recognize this, a whole range of animate and inanimate objects can be seen as "bait" in an extended sense of the word. For instance, almost all birds and mammals require a source of water, and a natural or man-made watering hole can be regarded as bait for the creatures in the immediate area. Many birds need sand or gravel to aid in their digestive processes, and such natural material can be spread out as bait. In a sense, a birdhouse is "bait" for cavity-nesting birds, and so is a supply of nest-building materials such as bits of string, yarn, or feathers. In the largest sense of the word, a correct habitat is probably the most effective "bait" of all, for it satisfies all a creature's physical needs for food, water, and cover. The back-yard birder often practices this kind of large-scale baiting by supplying birds with food, water, sand or gravel, nest-building materials, cavity boxes for nesting or roosting, and plantings of shrubs and trees for both food and cover. The birders who make these efforts are actually engaging in rather complete habitat management, even if only within a small physical space, and most are delighted with the results. Similar if less thorough habitat management can be practiced almost anywhere space is available, from a tiny plot up to many square miles of a game preserve or national forest. Many rural landowners and farmers are now recognizing the practical as well as aesthetic value of wildlife and are devoting strips or plots of their land to planned wildlife habitat. Again, most state game commissions or state universities can supply practical suggestions for local areas. A recent book, *Gardening with Wildlife*, by the National Wildlife Federation, offers a wealth of information to the homeowner interested in attracting birds and other wild creatures to his land. Ordering information can be obtained from the National Wildlife Federation, 1412 16th St. N.W., Washington, D.C. 20036.

Calling with sounds

It is possible to call birds and mammals with sounds. The sounds may be generated by a wide variety of techniques. Our understanding of how calling works can be helped considerably by looking briefly at some behavioral mechanisms in birds and mammals relating to territoriality, mating, and aggression. What follows is merely a simple account of these mechanisms, using a handful of species for illustration. In the natural world these mechanisms show a much greater variety.

Territoriality, mating, and aggression. Most birds and mammals have regular and predictable breeding cycles. With a majority of North American land birds, breeding commences in the spring, and may recur during the summer; most small mammals also commence breeding in the spring, but larger mammals may breed during the autumn. In all cases, the breeding cycle is timed so that the young enter the world at the time of maximum food availability—usually the spring or summer. During the breeding and young-rearing phases of their lives, birds and mammals generally exhibit behavioral responses that we associate with the phenomenon known as *territoriality*.

Territoriality serves several functions, including regulating population numbers and selecting the fittest males for breeding stock. Generally, territoriality works as follows. As the breeding season begins, males "stake claims" in the choicest habitat areas. Naturally, competition is keenest over areas of the best habitat, and normally the strongest, healthiest, most aggressive males succeed in driving off all competition, each claiming an area which then becomes "his" territory. The next most aggressive males take the next best territories, and so on down the line to the weakest and least aggressive males, who may be able to claim no territory, or at best ones that are so marginally suitable that they will attract no females. In this way the weaker, less aggressive males are in effect eliminated from the breeding stock, thus ensuring a healthy, strong population in the next generation.

Most males seem to require a territory that exceeds certain minimal dimensions. If they cannot claim a large enough territory, they will continue to compete with other males in an effort to carve out a larger area. If a species population is too numerous for the available habitat, only a few of the most aggressive males will be able to claim a large enough territory and settle down to breed; the remaining males will spend inordinate amounts of time fighting for space, and so successful breeding or rearing of young will not take place. Thus the population will be held in check and prevented from a disruptive expansion beyond the carrying capacity of the habitat.

Territoriality associated with reproduction varies widely in duration among different species, depending on the dynamics of young-rearing. Among wild turkeys and deer, for example, the males claim a territory and breed with several females, but then the mating and territorial urges dwindle rapidly and the males leave the rearing of young entirely to the females. On the other hand, foxes and most songbirds exhibit a different pattern; each male claims a territory, takes a single mate, and "keeps" the territory through other phases of the reproductive cycle as he helps his mate raise and care for the offspring. Turkey and deer, then, will exhibit the very high order of reproductive territoriality during only a single phase of the species' reproductive cycle, while foxes and songbirds will exhibit it over several phases, usually until the offspring are capable of some degree of self-sufficiency.

During the time when the male claims a reproductive territory, he acts out set behavior patterns that announce his claim to all other members of his species. In effect, he marks the boundaries of his territory in some way that says to other males of his species, "Private Property: Keep Out." Many birds proclaim their territories by regularly singing along the perimeters. Mammals often mark boundaries with scents from urine or musk, sometimes accompanied by scrapings, scratchings, or other visible signs. Whenever another male of the same species crosses these boundaries, the owner will defend his claims in a flurry of anger and indignation, offering everything from intimidating gestures to physical attack until the intruder withdraws, or, rarely, drives the defender off and claims the territory for himself.

Though many North American birds and mammals exhibit some degree of territorial behavior throughout the year, it is during the phase of high-pitched territoriality associated with the breeding cycle that a human can have the greatest success in attracting animals with typical breeding calls. The principle is simplicity itself. You merely go into a habitat used by a species and issue the call of the male of the species. The male who claims the territory will usually respond immediately, arriving all indignant over what he interprets as the intrusion of another male into his property. (A variation is sometimes used with polygamous species such as the wild turkey, in which the breeding call of the male is answered by the female with a call indicating that she is receptive to breeding. The female's calls can be imitated by a human to lure the male, who will arrive with amorous intentions.)

Calling breeding birds with sounds. I have found that calling birds during the mating season produces more reliable results than calling mammals, but that may be because I have more experience with calling birds. At any rate, bird calls are very easily reproduced in the field through the use of a portable tape recorder. The territorial songs of North American birds have been recorded and issued by the Cornell Laboratory of Ornithology, both as LP discs and as cassette tapes. These are available from several sources listed at the end of this book. If you are interested in calling a particular species, you can easily transcribe several minutes of its songs onto a blank cassette and replay them in the field, at the proper time of year and in the proper habitat, of course. If a breeding male is present, he will usually approach to investigate. Just how close he will approach depends upon the individual bird's safety zone, upon its motivational level, and also upon your ability to appear unintimidating. It is usually worthwhile to make repeated tries in several different places, thus increasing the odds of finding an individual bird that will respond really well to the calls.

Note: Repeated calling of birds can have a disruptive effect on the breeding cycle, similar to too much pressure from competing males. Ornithologists point out that if numbers of birders stream to the site of a breeding bird and use tapes in order to locate it, the breeding pair may abandon the nest, as has been reported recently on several occasions. A good rule of thumb, probably, is that a breeding bird should not be called more frequently than every third day, and then only briefly. Even this much frequency, however, should be avoided with rare or endangered species, which should be investigated only by management personnel or trained ornithologists. Note also that the use of tape recorders or other electronic devices to call game birds for hunting purposes is illegal in most states and is decidedly unsportsmanlike in any case. A wide variety of manual calls are available to hunters who wish to call game birds.

Calling breeding mammals with sound. Opportunities to call mammals with sound are fewer because most mammals during the breeding season use scent, not sound, to demarcate their territories. We will discuss scent as a calling device in a later section. But there is considerable interest among hunters in some regions in calling moose, elk, and deer. Manual calling devices for these species are sold by Herters, Inc., Waseca, Minn. 56093, with detailed instructions. The idea is to imitate the call of a male and elicit a territorial response from the male who claims the area. Similar calls for a limited number of other species are sold by several suppliers, but their use, in my experience, does not appear to be very widespread.

An interesting variation on the use of sounds in calling deer, used predominantly in the Southwest, is the practice known as *antler rattling.* The procedure is as follows. The practitioner takes two pairs of deer antlers into breeding-buck territory, conceals himself in an area of thick vegetation or high boulders, and attempts to reproduce the sounds of two buck deer fighting. He bangs the antler racks together and shuffles his feet on the ground to simulate the play of hooves. These noises are kept up for two or three minutes. The purpose is to fool a buck into thinking that his territory has been invaded by not one, but *two* interlopers. According to widely published reports, antler rattling can have two spectacular results: It can bring an aroused buck bounding right in almost on top of the rattler; and it can result in the rattler being shot if an overeager hunter happens upon the commotion going on behind the shrubbery.

Calling breeding mammals with scents

Among birds, songs and calls play a vital signaling role in breeding behavior; among mammals, the comparable signaling functions are often accomplished by odors. Among each species each sex has a characteristic odor. These odor signals can communicate over great distances in the proper atmospheric conditions and can trigger powerful behavioral responses in both sexes. A male, scenting another male, may become violently aggressive. After mating, females may become as keenly territorial as any male, claiming a territory that is either hers alone or hers in co-ownership with her mate, depending on how the family is structured in the species, and then defending it viciously against encroachment by strange members of the same species, regardless of sex.

Years ago it was not unheard of for someone to domesticate a female wild mammal and then, when she came into breeding condition, to stake her out as "bait" to bring others of the species in to the gun or trap. This was a costly operation, however, because the creature's breeding condition lasted only a few days out of the year and was often seasonally mistimed as a result of domestication, and, besides, the captive animals had the nasty habits of escaping at critical times, or, failing that, of pining away and dying. Modern science has now duplicated the sexual scents of wild mammals and conveniently packaged them in plastic squeeze bottles. The scents are claimed by the manufacturers to be irresistible to the target animals—most commonly deer, but also the smaller furbearing mammals sought by trappers.

Do these scent "lures" really work? Opinions are starkly divided. Some users swear by them; others dismiss them as useless. Actually, the truth is hard to establish in the wild, where any kind of standardized controls are difficult to maintain. My father has attempted an experiment of sorts on white-tailed deer. During two seasons of still-hunting he spent about equal amounts of time with and without the use of artificial scent lures. This was admittedly an open-ended experiment with many uncontrolled variables, and the conclusions must be regarded as tentative. To sum up, he was able to conclude (a) that commercial preparations appear to have no negative effect; (b) that some preparations may have some positive effect, though this may result from the preparation's masking human scent rather than functioning as an active lure; (c) that ordinary anise oil, long recommended in hunting lore, seemed to be the most effective scent used and appeared to be superior to commercial "lure" preparations.

What is the explanation for the apparent effectiveness of anise oil? We're not really sure. Is it, by virtue of its chemical properties, an unusually effective mask for human odors? Does it attract deer the way catnip attracts cats? (Anise is known to attract black bears and horses, but its effect on deer appears to be undetermined.) Is there some other explanation? We can't say. We can only say that it *appears* that white-tailed deer will approach closer to a human wearing anise oil than to one not wearing it, other things being equal. But this may be a local phenomenon. It seems entirely reasonable that animal odors differ from one geographical region to another where soils and vegetation differ, just as human odors change noticeably with changes in diet. An individual interested in using scent lures would probably do best to experiment with various preparations, including those recommended in the hunting lore of his region, and determine for himself what, if anything, seems to have real value.

The reader is probably aware of several traditional methods of attempting to minimize or mask human odors. One very old method was to give all hunting clothes a thorough washing, followed by a lengthy outdoor airing to remove as much human scent as possible. The clothes were then impregnated with a strong outdoor odor by burying them in a box of leaves or hay, or sawdust from an aromatic wood such as cedar. My friend Stuart Washburn tells me that in a section of New York State, crushed apples are used to mask human odors from deer; before starting afield, a hunter will rub his bootsoles with a ripe apple and perhaps crush another apple to release the odors near a still-hunting site. Other methods are followed in different parts of the country.

Decoys

Decoys can be employed to trigger responses in a number of bird species. The responses range from aggression associated with territoriality to the gentle flocking behavior exhibited by birds that live in social communities. The use of decoys to lure ducks and geese is widely known. Perhaps less well known is the use of decoys for shorebirds such as yellowlegs and plovers. Some of the decoys used were really only silhouettes—cutouts made from a plank and supported by a single stake driven into the sand or mudflat. Since the decoys were seen from the side by birds on the ground, the lack of a three-dimensional body was of little consequence. As with ducks and geese, the decoys were used to simulate birds at a feeding site and were usually supplemented with calls issued from a nearby blind. Shorebirds are no longer legal game, of course, and shorebird decoys are now almost nonexistent (except as antiques), but apparently they are effective and could be used with good results for legitimate nonhunting purposes.

Decoys can trigger violently aggressive responses among breeding land birds. A replica of a male bird introduced into an occupied territory will sometimes trigger an attack, and male robins have been known to attack stuffed and mounted robins and literally tear them apart. A variation of the actual replica is to introduce a mirror in which the male can see and attack his own image. Many territorial songbirds discover their images in house windows or other reflective surfaces and spend hour after hour, day after day, hopelessly trying to drive away the "intruding" male, often working themselves into exhaustion. A person can solve the problem by covering or removing the reflecting material. Among game birds, grouse are said to be particularly aggressive toward their own images discovered in mirrors placed near their drumming sites.

Decoys of predatory birds will trigger mobbing responses in a number of other bird species. A decoy of a great horned owl, for instance, if set in the right place, will frequently elicit a swarming attack from a flock of crows, especially if the decoy is used in conjunction with a crow call. Many songbird species will vigorously mob decoys of smaller owls such as the screech owl. Songbirds from all over the immediate area will gather to gang up on the owl and scold it with cries and chirps. Live predators may also serve as decoys. When I carry a hawk on my fist into woods or fields I am constantly surrounded by chirping and mobbing birds, and recently whenever I went near a kestrel nest I was sure to be the object of several near-miss vertical swoops by an angry, chattering female falcon, her flight feathers hissing against the wind like speeding arrows as she attempted to drive away the red-tailed hawk I was carrying. In the woods a carried hawk's presence will sometimes elicit an investigative flight by a Cooper's hawk, sharp-shinned hawk, or owl. Presumably a live bird is a more effective decoy than a wooden model, but the fact is that lifeless decoys do work, and they are certainly much easier to maintain and keep clean.

Calls that appeal to social behavior

Among a few species of birds and mammals, individuals beyond the family unit group together to form social communities during all or part of the year. Sometimes the groups are merely loosely knit collections with no distinct territory, as with wandering groups of winter birds or occasional small packs of free-ranging coyotes. Sometimes the groups occupy fairly well-defined ranges, as with wild turkeys or wolves; in other instances they may be tied to very exact geographical locations, as with swifts or prairie dogs, for example. Regardless of how the group dynamics operate, during the "social season" members of these species exhibit an impulse toward gregariousness, a need to associate with other members of the same species. Most communicate with sound, usually calls. The calls can be imitated by a human and can be used either to locate or attract members of the species.

The calling of ducks and geese to decoys is partly an appeal to their social responses, for these birds seem to enjoy feeding in flocks. Other game-bird species that can be called include turkeys, quails, and doves. Presumably most species of flocking birds could be somewhat interested by flocking calls issued in their immediate vicinity.

A few mammals, too, can be interested by social calls. Among the best known, no doubt, are wolves and coyotes, both of which signal other members of their packs by barks and howls. Howling is a very efficient way for a straggling individual to establish the whereabouts of the rest of the pack, and, conversely, for the pack to call to a strayed individual or pair. Wolves, once almost extinct in the contiguous states but now thankfully on the way back, will howl in response to a siren of the type used in police cars and ambulances. Recordings of these are available in some novelty shops; however, since wolves are dangerously few in numbers, they should not be unduly harassed or interfered with. I have heard howling coyotes appear to respond to my own voice imitations of their howls. Generally, imitated howls can be used to locate wolves or coyotes, but not to attract them.

Most mammals probably have communicative calls that are used within the family unit, and these no doubt present possibilities for exploration. I was recently surprised, for example, to learn that muskrats will respond to a call. I was doing a spring breeding-bird census, working along a creek bottom and calling birds by "squeaking" to imitate their distress calls (discussed below), when a young muskrat came drifting down the stream a few feet away. When I made another distress call I was startled to hear the muskrat answer with a similar sound; it then turned and swam back upstream to investigate. When I repeated the calls they had a definite attraction for it and it would frequently answer, and we had quite a little conversation before it finally lost interest and swam away. In imitating the calls of social mammals, however, one should remember that many of the calls are "danger" signals, warnings to the rest of the community of a nearby threat. Imitating these calls, of course, will reverse the effect desired by an observer.

Calling predators

Predators must capture and kill victims day after day in order to stay alive. Consequently they become thoroughly familiar with the distress calls and death cries of their prey species. Predators also practice a form of brigandry, with the larger, more aggressive species eager to rob smaller predators of their kills. Thus, in theory at least, imitating the distress calls of common prey species should attract every predator in the area interested in a free meal. Herters, Inc., Waseca, Minn. 56093, markets a series of predator calls designed to imitate the distress cries of small birds, rabbits, and mice. George Leonard Herter's *Professional Predator Calling Manual*, available from the firm, claims that the calls are effective on twenty species, including "red fox, gray fox, coyotes, wolves, bobcats, ringtail cats, mountain lions, grizzly bears, Kodiak bears, javelinas, wild boars, lynx, wolverines, jaguars, leopards, African lions, tigers, hawks, owls and eagles." Herters publishes a number of testimonials on the effectiveness of their predator calls. My own experience with them has been less satisfactory. I suspect that geographical differences may play some role in this and that predator calling may be more effective in some areas of the country than in others.

Calling birds by appealing to their mobbing instincts

For sheer fun and pleasure, one form of animal calling, in my opinion, stands above all the rest. It is simplicity itself, requiring no elaborate equipment, skill, or effort; and yet aside from its pleasure value it also has for the serious birder definite practical value. It is the technique of calling passerines, or small perching birds, by appealing to their mobbing instincts.

The mobbing response has already been mentioned in relation to decoys. But it can also be triggered by simple sounds which suggest to nearby birds (a) that a fellow passerine has fallen victim to a predator and is screaming in terror; (b) that a passerine has spotted a predator and is sounding the alarm by scolding; or (c) that a raptor is present and issuing its own distinctive call. All three classes of sounds can be made by humans, either unaided or with the aid of portable tape recorders. Any one or combination of them triggers the mobbing responses of the birds within hearing, and they will collect around the site of the noise, chirping, scolding, searching intently for the suspected predator. To some people this behavior seems illogical, for it appears that the birds are inviting disaster by coming into the vicinity of a dangerous killer. But such is not the case. The mobbing calls alert every bird in the area to the potential danger and point out the exact spot. Further, the mobbing serves to irritate the intruding predator and perhaps drive it away. And, finally, mobbing provides a measure of safety from a predator because, as studies have shown, a predator is much more likely to be successful in pursuit of a single quarry than in pursuit of a group of quarry, just as you or I would be more likely to catch one tennis ball thrown to us than four or five tossed at once. Mobbing thus serves, among other things, the same protective function as flocking among birds, herding among mammals, and schooling among fish.

The simple distress or pain call of a passerine is easily imitated by noisily kissing the knuckles of the hand or fist. The duration of the noise should be as prolonged as possible. With practice, some people can make the noise simply by pursing the lips and sucking air between them. This high-pitched, squealing sound closely approximates the sound of a passerine in the clutches of a hawk, owl, cat, or some other predator. I have seen starlings emit the sound merely at the presence of a snake near their nesting sites. Other birds hearing the sound will quickly gather to mob the alleged enemy.

The alarm or scold calls can be imitated in two ways. One is to place the tip of the tongue forcibly against the roof of the open mouth just above the upper teeth and then quickly pull the tongue backward to make a "chip" sound similar to the alarm note of many passerines. But a better sound, at least in my experience, is the much louder scolding call of a wren. This is made by attempting to pronounce the word "push" without making a vowel sound and greatly prolonging the "sh" sound at the end. In writing, it might look like this: "p-shhhhhhhh, p-shhhhhhhh, p-shhhhhhhhhhh, p-shhhhhhhhh." A good way to perfect the sound is to listen to a wren scolding and then imitate it as best you can. Some callers omit the "p" sound at the beginning and simply make a "shhhhhhhhh" sound as if telling a child to be quiet.

The third sound, that of a predator calling, is most effectively produced by playing a tape recording of a screech owl (Eastern or Western species, depending upon location). Tapes of the calls are easily made from commercially available recordings. Some people with great virtuosity in whistling can reproduce the sound very convincingly without tapes, but I prefer a tape for this reason: While playing the screech-owl call, one can also imitate the scold note of a wren and throw in a few distress calls here and there as well, and the combination of these sounds is dramatically more effective than any one issued alone.

The best technique is to find a suitable habitat and locate a small open area where the birds can be easily seen and plenty of perches are available. Then stand quietly, avoiding any sudden moves. If you're using a tape recorder, switch it on; in any case, begin making the "p-shhhhhhhh" wren notes and every thirty seconds or so give a distress call. Many people who have never seen this done cannot believe what may happen within the next few minutes. Numerous birds of many species will congregate in the bushes or trees around the noise, all chirping and scolding and peering about for the predator. Some will perch on branches only a foot or two from an observer's face, and I have had chickadees flutter only inches from my nose. Success depends, of course, on there being birds within the vicinity of the calls and nothing being done to frighten them away. Calling where there are no birds nearby will result in a big zero, for passerines do not travel very far to mob an enemy.

In my experience, mobbing activities usually reach a peak after about two to five minutes of calling, may last for two or three more minutes, and then begin to taper off as the birds' attention spans are exhausted. When this occurs it may be desirable to move on to another spot and begin anew, perhaps attracting an entirely new cast of mobsters.

The use of taped screech-owl calls has revolutionized the techniques of censusing passerine populations, because it brings into view many birds that would otherwise be unseen by fieldworkers attempting to cover a large territory in a limited time. Since the advent of tapes, bird population figures in all areas have leaped upward in annual census counts, not because there are more birds, but because more of them are being seen. The effect has been felt both in the number of species appearing in area counts and in the numbers within each species. The use of tapes is being called into question, however. It has already been mentioned that taped territorial songs and calls used during the breeding season can cause birds to abandon their nests or distract them from their young-rearing duties, which may seriously endanger the young. The same effect has been suggested when predator calls are used to census breeding birds. Another criticism is that taped predator calls may be an undesirable disturbance to birds at any time, exciting them unnecessarily and pumping too much adrenaline into their blood. This is a possibility, but at this time too little is known about it to justify a firm conclusion either way. A more widely accepted idea, especially within the scientific community, holds that taped calls that arouse the mobbing response may be dangerous if the activity interferes with the feeding behavior of birds who are on a restricted time/energy budget. This situation occurs whenever the birds are pushed to gather a certain minimum number of food-calories within a given time in order to maintain a normal metabolic level for themselves or their young. These circumstances can arise when adults must feed both themselves and their young, of course, but also when extremely cold temperatures force the birds to eat almost constantly during daylight hours in order to fuel their high metabolic rates and prevent hypothermia and death, especially during long winter nights. Many laymen find this notion difficult to accept, but it is widely held by wildlife experts. My own feeling is that taping is relatively harmless during periods of ordinary weather and abundant food supply, but that it should not be used during the breeding season or times of extreme cold (especially winter storms) except with extreme care and circumspection. As more evidence comes in, however, we may have to accept the fact that taping is undesirable under any circumstances, and be prepared to accept a moratorium on it if this is indeed the case.

In the Southeast where I do most of my birding, the use of tapes has become so commonplace that the badge of an active birder is just as much his tape recorder as it is his binoculars. Tapes are played on casual walks as well as on censuses and on trips made to remote places to find life-list rarities. Almost everyone carries his recorder and tapes in a homemade cloth cover fitted with shoulder straps so that the recorder hangs conveniently from the shoulder at waist level. Most prefer to use a small, light player even though the quality of sound reproduction cannot equal a larger recorder with bigger speakers. I have a miniature recorder made by Panasonic, model RQ-212 DAS, which works satisfactorily in the field and is small enough to fit inside a coat pocket. A model of similar dimensions is made by Sony. The ultraminiature players, some of which are cigarette-pack size, are unsuitable for calling purposes because of severely limited volume and reproduction quality.

IX

BLINDS

A blind, or "hide" as it is called in Britain, is a space where the occupant is obscured or concealed from view. Some blinds are entirely natural, consisting of landforms or patterns of vegetation; others are constructed by rearranging natural materials; still others are constructed of man-made materials; and some are combinations of these. This chapter will look first at blinds best suited to casual observation, hunting, and gunstock photography; and then at some blinds best suited to prolonged, systematic observation and tripod photography.

BLINDS FOR CASUAL OBSERVATION, HUNTING, AND GUNSTOCK PHOTOGRAPHY

Natural blinds

The wildlife enthusiast abroad on foot often needs the concealment of a blind in order to study, hunt, or photograph his quarry successfully. He can easily make use of simple, natural blinds such as tree trunks, boulders, streambanks, ravines, brushy vegetation, and so on. Since using these blinds is merely a common-sense matter of hiding behind something already existent, little needs to be said on the subject. It is useful to remember, though, that a blind of this type is most effective if located in deep shadow and, as seen by the animal, set against a dark background. A background of skylight or strong backlighting will silhouette the person using the blind and make his movements instantly noticeable. Further, a hunter or gunstock photographer using this type of blind will usually be required to have his equipment protrude forward of the blind in order to achieve a clear aim; thus any movement of the equipment will be in full view of the quarry. Detection of this movement can be minimized by (1) moving only when the animal is in a position where it cannot see the movement; or (2) moving so slowly that the animal is not frightened by what it sees. Usually the first alternative is the safest.

Simple constructed blinds

Sometimes circumstances permit the construction of a simple blind that will have advantages over a natural blind. One important advantage is that the user can locate it in the most desirable spot, not only with regard to lighting, but also with regard to its field of view. Generally speaking, the blind should not be in an open space, but rather in an area of thick vegetation or rough-hewn landforms where it will be less conspicuous. It should look out onto a relatively open area so the hunter or photographer can get a clear aim. Some typical good sites might be in a border of trees along a clearing or open forest area, or among bushes growing near a watering hole. The location should also take into account wind direction and thereby avoid wind-borne scents being carried to mammalian quarry.

Another advantage of a constructed blind is that it offers better concealment than many natural blinds. However, it should be obvious that most simple blinds do not conceal, but merely obscure the user from an animal's vision, and the user should keep his movements to a minimum. We should also note that simple blinds often require the cutting of shrubs, seedlings, or tree limbs. Such activity is illegal on much public and private land, and even if not forbidden by law it may be undesirable. Cut vegetation only if it is legal to do so and be especially careful not to destroy valuable growth. Cut only trash or nuisance brush or deformed saplings with no commercial value.

A basic type of simple blind may be constructed by the following method, which is appropriate anywhere but is particularly well suited for areas of low-growing brush or coniferous forestation. Select a stump, small bush, rock, or log that offers some concealment; then cut several shrubs or small saplings and "plant" them in a line or semicircle to improve the concealment offered by the natural object. The cutting may be accomplished with a sturdy knife. A shrub or small sapling may be grasped with the free hand near the base and bent to the horizontal; downward pressure of the knife blade against the apex of the bend will sever the wood easily, with the forces in the bent wood aiding the cutting force of the blade. Because the shrub is severed with a slanting cut it is already provided with a sharp point that may be pushed easily and securely into the ground. If small trees are not abundant, the lower limbs of larger trees can be used. Several pieces of vegetation can be arranged to provide a very effective screen that blends naturally into the surroundings. The ideal is a screen thick enough to provide good concealment, but open enough for good observation outward.

Once the screen is built, the floor can be prepared. All debris such as dry leaves and twigs that might make noise should be removed simply by kicking it to one side. A waterproof canvas or plastic groundcloth adds comfort if the ground is cold or damp. If the blind is tall enough, an elevated seat can be provided in the form of a flat rock or a slab from a decaying log. Such a seat is well worth its trouble, for it greatly increases the user's comfort during a long wait.

A variation of the above blind may be more practicable in hardwood areas. Poles in the form of fallen limbs or dead saplings may be tied horizontally between the trunks of two or three trees about thirty inches above the ground to form either a straight line or a wide V, depending on how the trees are spaced. Then fallen or cut limbs can be leaned against the poles from the front side of the blind, with the base of the limbs on the ground. This lean-to material should be fairly brushy in appearance, perhaps retaining a few dead leaves. The screen thus formed can be augmented with vines or evergreen boughs, but not to the point of making the blind form a sharp visual contrast with its surroundings. The leaves on the floor of the blind can be kicked into a pile at the base of the screen, thereby increasing its effectiveness. A groundcloth and seat can be provided as desired.

Variations of the above two blinds can be adapted to almost any kind of terrain with suitable vegetation. They are usually built on short notice to meet the demands of a particular occasion, but they can also be constructed for use on a recurring, more or less permanent basis and are quite appropriate for use near trails, watering holes, feeding sites, etc. When intended to be used throughout a season, the *sunken blind* or *pit blind* variation is sometimes used. In this type the same kind of screen is employed, but the floor of the blind is lowered by digging the kind of pit known in the military as a foxhole. The floor of the pit should slant to one side, where a sump hole provides drainage. Other niceties can include wooden shoring around the walls, a rack floor for protection against water, permanent seats, and stands to hold equipment. Pit blinds are most feasible where soil is light and porous enough to provide easy digging and good drainage.

Note: In hunting season, blinds such as the above may be hazardous to your health unless used with the back of the blind completely open so the occupant is fully exposed to view and recognizable as a human being. Strips of blaze-orange tape are strongly recommended for the occupant's back or the rear side of the blind material. If you're in a blind that is built so you're completely surrounded by natural-looking vegetation, time's winged chariot may appear undetected at your back in the guise of a dim-witted hunter with the urge to shoot any obscure thing that moves.

Simple artificial blinds

I know some hunters and photographers who use "instant" blinds created by stretching camouflage netting between two or three trees. The seeming simplicity of this is very attractive, but generally I prefer the real advantages offered by more stable materials. If suspended netting is touched even slightly the entire expanse of cloth waves like a flag and is sure to attract the attention and arouse the suspicion of any but the blindest quarry. It is almost impossible to insert a gun or camera lens through slits in the net without touching it sooner or later, usually sooner. The alternative is to work over the top of the net, but then the equipment and the user's head and shoulders are exposed to view, and he has nothing to rest his equipment against except the rope suspending the net. I find that I can crouch behind a stump, log, or rock, rest my equipment on top of it, and achieve a steady aim that can be maintained almost indefinitely, and still expose less of myself to the animal's view than is possible with a suspended net. A different use of netting in Europe is described by J. M. Baufle and J. P. Varin in their book *Photographing Wildlife.* According to them, if a gunstock photographer assumes a prone position and simply pulls netting over himself like a blanket, many wild creatures seem less fearful and wary of his presence.

Another type of "instant" blind is favored by predator hunters in the Rocky Mountain States. It is made by bending ordinary chickenwire to form a small four-sided enclosure in which the occupant may sit or kneel. The front side is lower than the back so the occupant's exposed head is set against a built-in background. The wire frame is covered with cloth that blends into the intended surroundings: white cloth for a snowscape, camouflage cloth for areas with vegetation, etc. The user may camouflage himself and his equipment with cloth of the same color. The blind, being very light, is easily carried in the hand; but because of its bulk it fits awkwardly if at all into an automobile and is best transported by pickup truck.

Tree stands

Another type of blind much used by deer hunters is the tree stand. This is merely a platform built in a tree a dozen feet or more above the ground. The platform, which is nailed securely to heavy limbs or suspended by sturdy braces nailed to the tree trunk, is usually about three feet square or larger, and above it are placed protective guard rails to prevent the occupant from absentmindedly stepping overboard. (A variation is the mechanical "climbing" seat which can be jacked up the trunk of a

Steps in building one type of simple blind. A pole is lashed between two trees. Vegetation is leaned against the pole from the front of the blind. Leaves and other debris are kicked to the front of the blind to provide a suitable floor. Various safety precautions are shown here. The back of the blind is left open so the occupant can be clearly seen and not mistaken for a game animal. (Normally, a blind such as this would have short sides to the left and right of the occupant to provide better concealment.) A blaze-orange cap hangs on the left tree and a red bandana handkerchief is pinned to the back of the hunter's coat as additional means of alerting other hunters who approach from the rear that here is a **human,** *not to be shot at.*

moderate-size tree. Advertisements for these can be found in the national hunting magazines and in the catalogs of sportsmen's supply houses.) The tree stand does not conceal the occupant behind a screen. Its effectiveness comes from its elevation, which places it above the line of sight of deer and other large ground-dwelling species that have no natural enemies that attack from above. Because these animals do not frequently look upward, the occupant of a tree stand is normally safe from visual detection unless the quarry is so far away that its cone of vision extends high enough to include the stand. Of course, most animals have peripheral vision that will pick up rapid or extensive movements in a tree stand, but if the occupant remains relatively motionless he has a good chance of remaining unseen. A further advantage of elevation is that air currents bearing the occupant's scent will normally pass well above animals on nearby ground. Tree stands provide useful vantage points not only for deer hunters, but for photographers and students of other animals as well.

Floating blinds

Floating blinds are sometimes employed when the quarry is associated with the water or water's edge. Though blinds are sometimes constructed on rafts, boats are the usual bases. Designs differ so radically that no attempt will be made here to give detailed plans. One approach calls for the erection of a wooden frame above the boat; cloth, or even a complete tent, is then stretched over the frame. Instead of cloth, wire mesh may be nailed to the frame and covered with reeds or other shoreline vegetation. Or a wooden frame may protrude only a short way above the gunwales and the entire top of the boat may simply be draped with camouflage netting. Or a simple screen of vegetation may be placed around the gunwales, leaving the top open. Numerous possibilities exist and are best selected with reference to the design of the boat and the habitat in which the blind will be used.

A typical tree stand of the type used by deer hunters in the Southeast. Many states now have laws prohibiting the driving of nails into forest trees, so check your local laws before constructing such a stand.

BLINDS FOR SYSTEMATIC OBSERVATION
AND PHOTOGRAPHY

Most of the blinds discussed in the previous section serve to obscure rather than conceal the user. By contrast, other types of blinds provide true concealment by completely enclosing the user inside four walls and a roof; yet paradoxically the user experiences a sense of freedom rather than confinement. Few people can forget the thrill of sitting in a photographic blind for the first time and watching some wild creature only a few feet away behaving as if the blind and observer did not exist. The observer feels during that initial experience that he has discovered something like the legendary cloak of invisibility and possesses almost magical powers over the denizens of the wild.

Unquestionably such blinds afford the best opportunity to observe, study, and photograph wild creatures at close range. Because the occupant is concealed from view he is free to move about, use binoculars, take notes, operate a camera—all without unduly disturbing his quarry, although the creature may at first be suspicious or wary if it detects human odors or noises of any kind coming from within. As a rule, however, animals will adjust even to these disturbances, accept the presence of the blind, and thereafter virtually ignore it.

At one time it was thought that in order to be effective a blind had to be camouflaged to look like a natural object. Centuries-old drawings of falcon-trapping operations in Holland show men using portable frames covered on the outside with hay to look like the haystacks which dotted the Dutch fields during the autumn migrations. Eric Hosking describes the work of the Keartons early in this century; they conducted bird photography from blinds elaborately disguised as tree trunks, cows, or sheep. Today we know that blinds need not be camouflaged to blend into the environment, because most animals respond not so much to form or color as to movement. One of the most effective blinds for wildlife observation, for example, is the archetypal product of industrial technology, the automobile. Nowadays, blinds are made of almost any suitable materials, including wood, metal, cloth, and plastic. Sometimes blinds are constructed of local materials and do blend naturally into the environment, but this is usually because of the convenience and adaptability of the materials, not because of a necessity to camouflage the blind from animals. However, it frequently is desirable to conceal a blind from the eyes of inquisitive humans, whose curiosity and investigations can seriously disrupt efforts to work with animals that are disturbed by a human presence.

The standard photographic blinds

Standard photographic blinds consist of a metal frame that dismantles for easy transport and a cloth covering with a closeable entrance and small ports for observation and photography. The size of the structure varies with the needs of the photographer(s). Professional movie photographers on assignment from a major studio may use wall tents large enough to serve also as living quarters. But a typical one-man blind is about three feet square and about six feet tall. It accommodates a photographer, tripod-mounted camera, comfortable seat, and amenities such as a lunch box and thermos. There are several types of one-man blinds, but the following seem especially popular.

Converted ice-fishing tents. One-man ice-fishing tents can be used as photographic blinds. Mike Hopiak, photographer for the Cornell Laboratory of Ornithology, uses several such blinds. His were purchased some years ago from Sears, Roebuck, Inc., but other outdoor suppliers in the northern states sell similar models. Mike modifies the tents in several minor ways, but the principal modification is to create ports for the camera lens by installing two-way zippers in the tent walls. The lens can be inserted through the opening and the zipper closed from both sides to prevent the quarry from seeing inside. The standard ice-fishing tent is covered with heavy canvas, which can be an advantage in cool or rainy weather but can be uncomfortable in warm climates where good ventilation is almost a necessity.

Custom-made blinds. For anyone requiring better ventilation or slightly more space than is provided by an ice-fishing tent, a homemade blind may be a good solution. Here are two popular methods of frame construction:

Aluminum angle may be used to construct a lightweight frame. The metal I use is manufactured by Reynolds Aluminum, whose products are stocked by many retail hardware stores. A blind three feet square and six feet high requires forty-eight feet of one-inch aluminum angle and sixteen small stovebolts with nuts. The aluminum is cut into three-foot

A photographic blind frame, without the cloth covering, constructed with telescoping tent poles. The cross braces at the top are lengths of aluminum angle. This detail photograph shows, in an exploded view, how the aluminum angle is attached to the poles. A wooden dowel is inserted into the pole and covered with a plastic cap; a threaded metal pin is inserted into the dowel, and the aluminum angle is simply drilled and fitted over the pin and held in place by a nut. The protruding portion of the pin provides a place to attach small guy ropes to anchor the blind against the wind.

lengths and the ends are joined, drilled, and fastened together with the stovebolts to form a frame that can be disassembled for easy transport. Complete, illustrated instructions for building this type of frame are contained in two Kodak publications, *More Here's How* (publication # AE-83) and *The Here's How Book of Photography* (# AE-100), both available through most camera stores and the latter through many libraries.

Telescoping tent poles can be used in place of aluminum angle to form the uprights for a frame. The poles are available from some sporting-goods stores and from tent manufacturers. In use, the poles are connected at the top by crossbraces that may be affixed to the poles in a variety of ways. My method is to insert a wooden dowel into the top of the pole and then drill the dowel and insert a metal pin. Four pieces of aluminum angle are then drilled to slip onto the pins to form crossbraces on all four sides.

There are advantages to both types of construction. The aluminum-angle frame, once assembled, is the more rigid. After being set up the entire blind can be easily picked up and moved about. It is probably the better suited for use as an elevated blind (discussed below). Its use is somewhat difficult on uneven terrain, however, because the rigid frame tends to tilt downhill. The telescoping-tent-pole frame has fewer parts and is faster to set up; but it has less rigidity and, once set up, is difficult to move. The variable length of the uprights, however, makes this design very useful on uneven or sloping terrain.

A cloth covering is placed over either type of frame. Opinions vary considerably over what material makes the best covering. Some prefer canvas or nylon tent cloth; others, dark muslin; and still others, burlap. I use burlap because the climate where I work is fairly warm and the coarse weave of burlap provides a degree of ventilation. A good bargain is the relatively inexpensive burlap that can be purchased from upholstery shops. Before this material is sewn it should be thoroughly soaked with a garden hose and allowed to dry in the open air. (Do not use a washing machine or laundry drier—the material will unravel.) This preshrinking will prevent difficulty later if the blind should get wet, and it also shrinks the material to an ideal width for a three-foot-square blind. Whatever the material used, it should be sewn to fit snugly over the frame to prevent its flapping in the wind, which would disturb most quarry. An objection frequently raised against a porous or thin cloth cover-

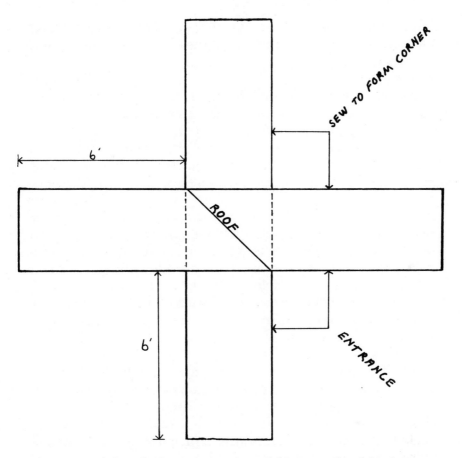

Diagram of the cloth covering for a photographic blind.
Two pieces of cloth, each five yards long, are crossed and
sewn together at three corners of the blind; the fourth corner
is fitted with a zipper or other fastening device to form the
entrance.

ing (such as burlap or nylon) is that it will allow direct sunlight
to pass through and cast the photographer's shadow on the
front of the blind, which will disturb the quarry. An easy solution to this problem, however, is to hang a dark cloth curtain
on the inside of the blind on the wall facing the sun. The curtain not only prevents those unwanted shadows, but also helps
keep the blind cool.

Construction of the cloth covering for the frames described
above is quite simple. Two lengths of material, each five yards
long and just over three feet wide, are crossed at the center to

form a cross, as illustrated, and sewn together. The area of double thickness will form the roof of the blind. Then the edges of three pieces of the overlapping cloth are sewn together, the seams coinciding with three corners of the blind. The fourth corner is left unsewn and becomes the entranceway. It is equipped so the blind can be closed from within by any of the following devices: a heavy-duty zipper (available from upholstery shops); safety pins; Velcro tape; or lacing eyelets. Once the entranceway is complete, all that remains is to cut small observation ports in the front and sides of the blinds, and ports for the camera lens wherever they are desired. Observation ports should be small—about an inch square—and covered on the inside with cloth flaps. Ports for the lens should be fairly large so the camera can be tilted or panned without undue interference, yet the opening should not allow the quarry to see inside the blind. Adjustable lens ports can be made by installing two-way zippers. Another solution is to fit a large cloth sleeve to the port on the inside of the blind. The free end of the sleeve can then be fitted with an elasticized cuff through which the lens can be inserted.

When used in the field, either of these blinds should be anchored in place by small but strong guy ropes running from the top of each corner to pegs driven firmly into the ground. Anchoring ensures that the blind will not topple in the wind, an event that is not only a nuisance to the photographer, but also may injure or kill helpless young quarry.

Elevated blinds

Photographers seeking to record birds at their nests must frequently elevate blinds to a considerable height above the ground in order to photograph tree-nesting species. The three most common ways of elevating blinds are by tree platforms, by construction scaffolding, and by pylons. Some photographers set up a standard metal-frame blind atop the elevated structure; others prefer to stretch the blind cloth over a part of the structure itself. No matter what method is used, an elevated blind should be erected in stages, over a period of days; otherwise the lives of the young birds may be imperiled (see the discussion in the next chapter of animal responses to photographic equipment).

A *tree platform* is a simple wooden floor anchored on a tree limb or limbs and braced against the tree trunk. This is the simplest way to elevate a blind, requiring the least amount of

A small permanent blind located on the Pea Island National Wildlife Refuge in North Carolina.

materials and effort. The ploy is rarely practicable, however, because birds seldom place nests in convenient relation to large, sturdy limbs footing on open areas of a tree. But occasionally they do, and then a platform may be the solution of choice.

Construction scaffolding of the type used by building contractors is preferred by many professional photographers as the most versatile and practicable means of elevating a blind. Some own their own scaffolding material; others rent it from contractors, who may agree to furnish truck transportation for the scaffolding and even labor to assemble the materials (for a fee, of course). The scaffolding should be anchored securely with guy wires or ropes.

Pylons are tall poles (often trees that have been felled and limbed for the occasion) planted in the ground like fence posts. Four pylons, crossbraced to one another and secured by guy ropes, serve to support a platform placed near the top. The pylon structure is usually braced to the nest tree so the two will sway in unison in the wind and the photographer will not have to constantly adjust the focus of his camera.

There are alternatives to elevating a blind. One is to elevate the camera, which is then controlled by the photographer from a blind on the ground. Special clamps for attaching cameras to tree limbs or man-made structures are available from most photographic-supply houses. Another alternative is to lower the nest (on its supporting limb) to a level suitable for ground-based or slightly elevated photography. This is a difficult and risky operation, requiring special equipment and techniques, and is suitable only for very limited circumstances. It should not be undertaken lightly. For a full discussion of the difficulties involved, see Eliot Porter's *Birds of North America: A Personal Selection.*

Permanent blinds

Some situations justify the building of permanent blinds. Here are three examples.

Like many of our national wildlife refuges, the Pea Island National Wildlife Refuge on North Carolina's Outer Banks is a year-round haven for birds, particularly aquatic species. Hundreds of people visit the refuge every month to enjoy the abundant bird life. The refuge managers have erected a permanent blind near a visitor's center. The blind is freely accessible to interested birders and photographers. It is also used by the refuge personnel to census birds and to operate cannon nets in trapping and banding programs. Because birds usually stay in the refuge for at least a season, they become accustomed to the presence of the blind and there is no necessity to camouflage its appearance; it resembles an outhouse more than anything else. Incoming birds soon ignore it completely. Similar structures are found at many refuges and parks open to the public.

*A permanent, camouflaged blind used in hawk-trapping
operations in Virginia's Blue Ridge Mountains.*

Another permanent blind is located in a small clearing on
the crest of Virginia's Blue Ridge. The site is used each autumn
by falconers and banders to trap migrating hawks. Since the
birds are merely passing through and are shy of human habita-
tions, the blind is somewhat camouflaged to lessen its resem-
blance to a "civilized" structure. It is also larger than the Pea
Island blind in order to accommodate the two, three, or four
people necessary to operate a hawk-trapping station. The skele-
ton of the building consists of heavy poles planted in the
ground; the exterior is weatherproof plyboard and tarpaper,
painted a dull gray, spotted with black, and scantily covered

with tree limbs. Observation ports are closed from the inside with cloth flaps. In this case, building a large, permanent blind proved more practicable than packing in two or three portable blinds each season across the difficult terrain leading to the site.

Still a third type of blind is exemplified by the observation room at the Cornell Laboratory of Ornithology. It is equipped with large plate-glass windows through which visitors may observe waterfowl on the laboratory pond and a variety of birds and mammals on the nearby trees and grounds. Live sounds are piped into the observation room from microphones positioned in the observation area. The animals have become accustomed to the observatory and pay no attention to the visitors, who may relax, look at exhibits, or move about freely to get a better look at some wild creature only a few feet beyond the glass.

Waterfowling blinds

It would appear to be an oversight not to mention waterfowling blinds, for their users constitute a numerous fraternity. However, probably a great majority of waterfowlers do not own or even live near wetlands, and so do not build their own blinds; rather, they purchase the right to use blinds built by someone else. Those who do own wetlands suitable for waterfowling are probably already expert on the subject of blinds or at least have a neighbor who is. It seems questionable, therefore, that a discussion of the rather complex subject of waterfowling blinds would be of any real value to the general readership of this book. Those seeking information can find several excellent books on the subject. I own and like *The North American Waterfowler*, by Paul S. Bernsen. It contains detailed, illustrated instructions for building several types of waterfowling blinds, aerial photographs that demonstrate the proper ways to select blind sites, and a good deal of information on other aspects of the sport. Another good book on the subject is *The Complete Wildfowler* by Grits Gresham.

X

WILDLIFE PHOTOGRAPHY

Many people who get involved with wildlife sooner or later want to photograph wild animals. There are many reasons for doing so. Photography may legitimately be considered a form of hunting and satisfies the hunting instinct; but the "trophy" is a photograph and the animal remains unharmed, freely roaming the earth to complete its natural life cycle. Photography also satisfies the aesthetic sense, first when the photographer sees the animal's beauty at close range as he photographs it, and again when he sees the developed film. At a still deeper level, difficult to articulate, photographing a wild animal forces the photographer into a unique psychological intimacy with the animal. He must know his quarry so thoroughly, study it with such intense concentration, and submit himself so completely to its natural routine, that he enters into a kind of personal relationship with it that is difficult to describe and probably can only be understood by one who has experienced it.

And of course wildlife photography also has educational value. Photographs enable people who have never seen a particular animal to experience it vicariously and to learn things about it that they would otherwise never have known. Photographs provide valuable records when used to document field studies in animal growth and development, food preferences, behavior patterns, and numerous other facets of the lives of wild creatures. Photographs can sometimes be worth more than the 10,000 words of the familiar cliché because a photographic image may reveal details that the human eye alone could never have registered.

Most successful wildlife photography involves using either advanced stalking techniques or blinds. It is possible to go stalking with a camera for shots at whatever animals one encounters by chance. This can be exciting and fun, but you cannot expect to get a great many photographs this way. Much better is to stalk a particular quarry whose territory, movements, and habits are determined beforehand. A blind may also be used for chance encounters if placed beside a trail, watering hole, or some other likely area; but again a more productive technique is to place the blind near a site that may be called a "control point" because it in some way dominates or controls a particular animal's behavior. Typical control points are nests, dens, watering holes, display and mating sites, sleeping sites, and perhaps other frequented areas within the animal's territory. Often a photographer can create a control point by providing a food or water supply that will be accepted and used by the quarry. This practice is disdained by purists, however, who prefer the greater challenge of finding and making use only of natural control points.

Photographing wild animals can involve a person in many pleasant hours spent outdoors searching for quarry and studying the best ways to deploy the blind and equipment. Since some of the more spectacular photographic subjects are found in unusual places, ingenious solutions are sometimes required to get equipment into position. Blinds must sometimes be floated on water, raised high into trees, or positioned on cliff ledges. The work can get adventurous and dangerous. But you can minimize the danger by using good judgment and following reasonable precautions; and there are so many birds and mammals who inhabit the ordinary, safe areas of the environment that a photographer never need take any risks at all.

Ordinarily, the person who is thinking of taking up wildlife photography is most concerned about the type of equipment he will need. This is a legitimate concern, and in the following pages an attempt will be made to survey basic kinds of equipment, to discuss the pros and cons of the various options, and to discuss in some detail the most common techniques for effectively employing the equipment. Throughout the discussion it is assumed that the reader is already familiar with the basic procedures for taking good photographs with a hand-held camera with adjustable controls. It is also assumed that he wishes to take what are generally regarded as "good" wildlife photographs. These would ordinarily be color transparencies (or occasionally black-and-white exposures) that are sharp, well composed, and properly exposed. A good still photograph would provide a portrait of the animal in its natural surroundings, and its image would occupy a sizable portion of the frame. A movie would depict the animal behaving normally in its environment, unaware of the photographer or camera. Photographs and movies that meet these basic criteria make enjoyable viewing for both the photographer and almost anyone else interested in wildlife, and occasionally may have commercial value.

STILL CAMERAS

The still-camera nature photographer today can choose among large, medium, and small formats. Large-format cameras use sheet film sized 4×5 inches or larger, the standard color film in the United States being one of the Ektachromes. With the notable exception of Eliot Porter, few wildlife photographers use this format any more because the camera is large, heavy, and slow to operate, and the film is expensive. Medium-format cameras use 120/220 or 70mm roll film, the standard color film in the United States again being one of the Ektachromes. Medium-format cameras have a number of adherents among wildlife photographers. But the most popular camera with both amateurs and professionals is the small-format 35mm single-lens-reflex (SLR). The camera itself is small, light, and easy to use; some brands can be equipped with a wide range of accessories and thus become amazingly versatile. The standard color films, being small, are relatively inexpensive and yield transparencies suitable for home viewing in a slide projector, for making color prints, or for reproduction by four-color printing processes. The films include not only the Ektachromes, but also the films that are widely regarded as having the greatest color fidelity and resolving power of any type available—the Kodachromes. These films can yield detailed enlargements up to thirty diameters that have no apparent grain at normal viewing distances.

Most wildlife photographers today, including many demanding professionals, feel that modern 35mm films are adequate for most purposes and that the convenience of the 35mm SLR makes this format ideal for nature work. There are advantages to large and medium formats, however, that should not be lightly dismissed, and so each will be discussed in turn. Let's begin with the 35mm SLR and then use it as a standard of comparison for the other two formats.

Small format: the 35mm SLR

The 35mm SLR combines light weight and portability with the basic advantage of through-the-lens viewing—that is, the user looks into the viewfinder and via a mirror and prism sees the world through the camera's taking lens. When the shutter is tripped the mirror swings out of the light path, a focal-plane shutter operates to expose the film, and the mirror swings back into viewing position. Through-the-lens viewing allows for the use of an almost infinite variety of lenses, because the pho-

Stalking can yield unexpected pictures, but has hazards. This spotted sandpiper was photographed when it suddenly appeared as I was walking slowly along a stream. The film was 35mm Tri-X, the lens 300mm; the camera was hand-held. What appear as shadows diagonally across the picture and across the bottom are actually pieces of vegetation close to

the camera that were blurred by the long lens' shallow depth of field. Though these flaws do not ruin the picture entirely, they do create distractions. This illustrates one of the most common problems in photographic stalking: the subject seldom appears in circumstances that afford the photographer a perfectly clear field of view.

Automobiles can serve as very effective photographic blinds. This song sparrow was photographed from a car parked near a garden stake after I noticed the bird frequently used it as a perch. This eastern kingbird was photographed after I drove my vehicle slowly up beside it as it perched on a fence along a country road. Both photographs on 35mm Tri-X with a 300mm lens; in both cases the camera was rested on a rolled-up jacket placed on the window ledge of the car.

tographer sees through the lens itself he has no difficulty in composing or focusing, whether using a wide-angle, telephoto, or extreme close-up lens. In addition, most modern SLRs come equipped with built-in light meters that couple with the aperture and shutter-speed controls, and some models even automatically adjust themselves for correct exposure. Some 35mm SLRs accept motor drives that automatically trip the shutter and advance the film and can be triggered either manually or by an electronic impulse.

Wildlife photography with a 35mm SLR divides easily into two main categories. The first is characterized by the use of natural light and a fairly long telephoto lens (300mm or longer). If stalking his quarry, the photographer may carry the camera hand-held or mounted on a gunstock; if working from a blind erected near some control point he will probably mount the camera on a tripod. Because telephoto lenses are "slow" (that is, have relatively small maximum apertures), one is at times forced to use a fast film such as High Speed Ektachrome in order to freeze motion or get sufficient depth of focus. Fast film necessarily has a coarse grain and low resolving power, but this itself can sometimes have a pleasing aesthetic effect. An alternative is to use a slow, high-resolution film such as Kodachrome and to expose only when the animal has momentarily frozen. This is not impossible to do if you study the animal for a while and acquire a sense of its natural rhythms.

The other category of photography is characterized by the use of a short telephoto lens (about 135mm) and, usually but not always, artificial light created by electronic flash. Successful photography of this type almost always involves using a blind situated near a control point. Strong flash units placed near the point will provide enough light to allow for the use of Kodachromes and a small lens aperture so that the greatest possible detail and depth of focus can be obtained. The brief duration of the flash freezes the motion of most animals. A successful photo of this type will usually reveal every hair or feather barb of the creature being photographed.

Both kinds of wildlife photography are greatly facilitated by a

Blinds located near feeding areas afford many photographic opportunities. This black skimmer was photographed from the blind at Pea Island National Wildlife Refuge, shown on page 189.

motor-drive attachment on the camera. With a motor-driven camera mounted on a gunstock and triggered by a cable release, you can easily track a moving animal with the right hand holding the gunstock to the shoulder and the left hand controlling the focusing knurl of the lens. The animal can be kept constantly in focus and never disappears from the viewfinder as a result of a fumble in advancing the film. The possibility of firing up to four frames per second increases the odds of catching the animal in an ideal pose during an action sequence, something that demands a great deal of luck when the camera is operated manually. A motor drive is also desirable when a camera has been set up near a control point and is operated from a distance by the photographer in a blind. To be sure, the noise of the motor drive will at first disturb the animals, but most soon come to accept it and may even ignore it; this is vastly more productive than the certain disturbance and delays created each time the photographer leaves the blind and moves toward the animals to advance the film manually. A motor drive is not essential to wildlife photography, but it enables the photographer to be more efficient by taking a greater number of pictures in a given amount of time.

There are many brands of 35mm SLRs suitable for our purposes, but my impression is that among serious photographers, Nikon cameras are the most popular choice. For some years I have scanned the picture credits in *Audubon, National Wildlife*, and other magazines featuring wildlife photography. A surprisingly high percentage of cover and inside photos have been taken with Nikon equipment by such well-known professionals as Frederick Kent Truslow, Les Line, Hope Ryden, John Dominis, Nina Leen, Larry West, Ann LaBastille, and others too numerous to mention. After using Nikon equipment for a few years I can see why it is a good choice. Optical and mechanical quality are excellent, and Nikon produces a full system of equipment, including a wide array of lenses, different camera bodies, motor drives, remote-control devices, etc. The entire line has a widely held reputation for ruggedness.

Medium format: the 2¼ cameras

Several manufacturers produce 2¼ cameras, both twin-lens (one taking lens, one viewing lens) and SLR models, that may be used for wildlife photography. But one 2¼ SLR is so especially suited for the task that we may as well go ahead and

*The basic Hasselblad 500 C/M camera with standard 80mm
lens. (Photo courtesy Paillard, Inc.)*

discuss it without further ado. It is a Swedish camera, the Hasselblad, reputedly developed by Dr. Victor Hasselblad because he wanted an ideal instrument for bird photography. It is small and light and can be equipped with numerous accessories, including a variety of lenses, a motor-driven body, remote-control mechanisms, and so on. Though developed for waist-level viewing, it can be equipped with a special prism for eye-level viewing and can be mounted on a gunstock. Hasselblad equipment is widely known for its high quality, and the lenses are manufactured by the famous West German firm of Carl Zeiss, Inc. Hasselblad equipment has a reputation for ruggedness that compares favorably with that of Nikon.

The major disadvantages and advantages of a Hasselblad over a 35mm SLR, as I see them, are as follows.

A Hasselblad is initially expensive, and the lenses, especially, are costly because the camera does not contain a focal-plane shutter and consequently each lens must be equipped with a built-in leaf shutter. The camera does not come equipped for eye-level viewing and the porro-prism necessary to convert it for that purpose is an additional cost. The larger film size (120, 220, or 70mm) is more expensive. Kodachromes are not available in these sizes.

Also a Hasselblad is not as easy to handle as a 35mm SLR. It is basically a waist-level camera and is shaped for that. The telephoto lenses are necessarily larger and heavier than those of a 35mm SLR. The basic camera does not have a through-the-lens metering system (though one can be purchased), nor does it have an instant-return mirror. The motor-driven model does return the mirror automatically, but not as quickly as does an ordinary 35mm SLR; the motor drive will operate at only about two frames per second, as compared to four or more for a Nikon.

On the other hand, the 2¼-inch (or 70mm) square format provides a considerably larger film area; consequently, to produce an enlargement with a minimum dimension of eight inches, 2¼ film needs to be enlarged less than four diameters as compared to eight diameters with 35mm film. The effect is a marked reduction in apparent grain and an increase in resolving power. This is very advantageous in natural-light photography using a high-speed, large-grained film such as High Speed Ektachrome, and it becomes especially important if the film is pushed beyond its normal ASA speed. The same advantages relating to grain and resolving power are realized with black-and-white films.

The Hasselblad is quieter, too. A focal plane shutter shouts; a leaf shutter barely whispers. The quiet Hasselblad between-the-lens shutter can be a distinct advantage when low noise levels are important. The motor-driven body can be equipped with a remote-release cord that trips the shutter but delays the motor operation as long as the photographer wishes. Additionally, the leaf shutter allows for flash synchronization at speeds up to 1/500 second, as compared to 1/60, 1/80, or 1/125 for most 35mm focal-plane shutters. This high speed allows for motion-freezing flash without danger of ghost images forming from ambient light, and for other advantages as well.

I do not own a Hasselblad, mostly because the expense of owning two systems is too great. I chose a 35mm system because it was initially less expensive, was more versatile overall, and seemed adequate for most situations. There have been times when I wished I had gone the Hasselblad route, and times when I was glad I hadn't. It's not an easy issue to resolve even for myself and I certainly would not attempt to resolve it for anyone else.

Large format: 4×5 and up

Large-format cameras come equipped to take sheet film in 4×5, 5×7, 8×10, and even larger sizes. Though it's possible to buy rangefinder and even reflex 4×5 cameras, undoubtedly the best type for wildlife photography is the 4×5 view camera. Since this format has only limited popularity, no discussion of the camera's basic operation will be given here; anyone wishing more information may refer to the bibliography at the end of the book. The major advantage of the format is, of course, the film size. Whenever I look at a reproduction of one of Eliot Porter's bird photographs or David Muench's landscapes I realize that not even Kodachrome in a small format can capture all the richness of detail that a 4×5 sheet of Ektachrome can. Black-and-white 4×5 film also seems richly detailed and almost grainless in normal reproduction sizes.

The view camera's bulk and time-consuming operation make it most suitable for the painstaking individual with almost unlimited time and patience and an uncompromising desire for quality. As for popular brands, so few wildlife photographers use these cameras that the question is meaningless.

Eliot Porter took many of his exquisite photographs with a Graflex view camera and a 180mm Zeiss Protar lens; neither the camera nor the lens is manufactured any longer. Several well-known brands of view cameras and lenses are available through dealers who cater to professional studio photographers.

Still photography from blinds

Blinds are among the still photographer's most vital pieces of equipment, and several kinds are discussed in another chapter. Photography from a blind divides easily into two basic forms.

First, the photographer may have the camera mounted on a tripod inside the blind with the lens looking through a port in the front or side of the blind. This is the usual technique with natural-light photography, for it allows the photographer to adjust the camera's exposure values to compensate for changes in the light falling on the subject area. It also allows him to make other adjustments such as changing the lens focus and changing the aim of the camera to follow moving animals or improve the composition of a scene. He may even change lenses without disturbing the quarry. Such adjustments are also useful when the camera is used in conjunction with flash units mounted outside the blind; the units may be set to illuminate a fairly large area, and a telephoto lens may then be used to narrow the camera's taking angle to the small portion of the illuminated scene occupied by the quarry. For this kind of work a sturdy tripod—the sturdier the better—is essential. It should have large, easily used adjustment controls that can be operated without noise. A camera inside a blind is usually tripped by a cable release to minimize camera movement. Ordinarily a motor drive would not be used in this mode of photography, though of course there are exceptions.

In the second major form of photography from a blind, the photographer mounts the camera on a tripod located outside the blind and triggers it by some form of remote release. This mode is restricted to circumstances in which the quarry is known from time to time to occupy a precise spot; only then can the camera be prefocused and can composition be judged in advance. The photographer observes the subject and trips the camera whenever the animal assumes a desirable pose. This technique is most frequently employed at bird nests and mammal den openings, and at feeding sites—areas of rather small physical dimensions in which the animal's appearance is predictable. This kind of photography is sometimes based on the use of natural light, but the initial setup of the camera may have to be modified if the light changes as a result of passing clouds or a change in the angle of the sunlight. This problem can be mitigated somewhat by the use of a camera with automatic exposure adjustments. Even with this advantage, however, care must be taken to avoid shadows from trees or other objects falling across the subject and ruining an otherwise satisfactory photograph.

Most often this mode of photography employs artificial illumination by electronic flash units. Superior lighting is achieved by using two units, one placed to either side of the camera, with the main flash unit higher than the camera and the secondary or fill unit about level with the lens. (Some photographers prefer three units—one main and two fills.) Whereas a single unit mounted directly on the camera will produce a flat, washed-out picture, multiple units used to the side of the camera yield natural-looking textures and modeling, and rich, saturated color. When flash is employed, any background area within the viewing angle of the lens that is not illuminated by the flash will appear dark or black in the resulting transparency. A black background can be aesthetically pleasing if it serves to focus attention on the subject and bring it into sharp relief; but it can also be objectionable if it is not artfully controlled, for it gives an artificial or unnatural appearance to the scene. Some photographers like to employ additional flash units specifically to provide even illumination over the background.

Flash units for wildlife photography should have a high light output if the goal is to use Kodachrome film and small lens apertures in order to get great depth of focus. The output of professional units is often rated in watt-seconds, but a more familiar popular rating is the guide number. A guide number is keyed to a given ASA film speed and provides a handy way of determining the correct lens aperture to use at a given flash-to-subject distance. To use a guide number, simply divide it by the distance in feet between the flash and subject, and the result indicates the correct lens opening. For example, I use a Metz 203 unit with a guide number of 92 for Kodachrome 25. To determine the correct aperture at a flash-to-subject distance of four feet, I divide 4 into 92, which yields 23; this is closest to f/22 on my lens aperture scale, and f/22 is, then, the indicated aperture to use, regardless of whether the camera itself is two or twenty feet from the subject. However, note that guide numbers are computed for using the flash indoors, where much of the light is reflected from walls and ceilings. For outdoor use the lens should be opened one f/stop above what is indicated by the guide number. So with my unit placed four feet from the subject, I shoot at f/16 and achieve dead-on exposure.

For a secondary or fill light I use a Mecatwin flash head. It draws its power from the same battery as the Metz unit, but because it has its own capacitors, it does not affect the light output of the main unit. This is an important feature to look for in a flash system. Some systems allow for the use of two or more flash heads, but employ only a single capacitor. As a result, the introduction of a second flash head reduces the output of the main light by 50 percent, the introduction of a third head reduces it by 67 percent, and so on.

The Mecatwin unit has a guide number of 64 for Kodachrome 25, which is the equivalent of one f/stop less output than the Metz. This is actually desirable for a second flash unit, for by placing it at the same distance as the main flash, it provides ideal fill light to soften the shadows produced by the main light, but does not destroy modeling. Setting the lamps up and computing the f/stop to be used is quite simple after a bit of experience. With any new flash equipment, however, it is always a good idea to run tests to determine a personalized, finely tuned guide number for the particular flash, lens, and film combination. More information on the use of flash units is available in books listed in the bibliography.

Special high-speed flash. Some photographers specialize in photographing unusually fast-moving subjects and wish to freeze the action with extremely high-speed flash. Photographs of hummingbirds in flight, with the extremely rapid wingbeats frozen to reveal crisp detail, for example, are in this category, and require flash with a duration as short as 1/30,000 second as compared to the 1/500 or 1/1,000 second duration of ordinary flash units. To my knowledge, no commercially available battery-powered flash units meet these requirements. However, I learned in a personal communication from Eric Hosking that schematics and parts for such units are available from EG&G, Inc., 35 Congress St., Salem, Mass. 01970. The parts must be assembled by a competent electronics specialist, and housings must be fabricated to hold the units. One of the officers of EG&G, incidentally, is Dr. Harold Edgerton, inventor of the electronic flash.

Remote release devices. The photographer who sets up his camera outside the blind must have some way of triggering the shutter from a distance. There are several ways of accomplishing this. For very short distances a long cable release may be employed. For longer distances a lever device, operated by a string and pulley, may be rigged to depress the shutter-release button. A lever arrangement is probably much better than the pneumatic squeeze-bulb release available from a number of manufacturers. In my experience the squeeze bulb has an unpredictable and inordinate delay time which renders it useless in photographing the smaller, more active wild creatures. A more sophisticated release is the battery-powered solenoid. Various models are available from Karl Heitz, 979 Third Avenue, New York, New York 10022. Solenoids must be carefully adjusted to prevent damage to the camera and may have to be mounted on custom-made holding brackets in order to be adapted to a particular model camera. The easiest remote releases to use are those available for motor-driven cameras such as Nikon and Hasselblad. The motor drives of both cameras have built-in solenoids which can be activated by an electric cord of considerable length, or by cordless radio command. Radio-control units are available from both manufacturers.

Automatic release devices. Automatic releases are used by a number of wildlife photographers. The releases are activated by an animal when it enters the focal area of the camera. Some releases are simple mechanical arrangements, such as a thread strung across a trail and attached to a simple pulley-and-lever arrangement that depresses the camera's shutter-release button. When an animal walks into the thread, the shutter is tripped, the thread breaks, and the animal goes on its way, hardly aware that anything has happened. If a solenoid is employed in place of a pulley-and-lever device, the thread must be attached to some kind of switch that will close a circuit and activate the solenoid. A common solution is to attach the thread to an ordinary spring-loaded mousetrap, and let the force of the trap throw a switch. The thread-across-the-trail technique works satisfactorily if the quarry is an animal large enough to apply the necessary force to the thread.

For very small mammals and for most birds, the most satisfactory technique is to use a solenoid activated by electronic sensing equipment. The most common type employs a photo-cell on which is focused a beam of light. The device is similar to those used in burglar alarms and automatic doors. When an animal interrupts the light beam, a circuit is closed and the solenoid activated. (Other less widely used types employ sensors which respond to pressure, sound, or proximity.) Photocell triggering devices make possible the instantaneous response necessary to photograph birds flying across the camera's field of view at very close ranges. I am not aware that any automatic releases are commercially available, but schematics and parts lists have been published in several electronics hobby magazines and the devices can easily be assembled by anyone with the necessary skills.

MOVIE CAMERAS

Still cameras provide finely detailed portraits but can give only a suggestion of an animal's movements. A movie camera can record motion; but the film must be kept traveling through the camera and cannot be locked as precisely in position as it can in a still camera, so it does not record comparable detail. Also, largely for economic reasons, the more popular movie cameras use smaller film formats: 8mm or 16mm. Only the very well-financed photographer can afford the expense of 35mm or 70mm cameras and the enormous amount of film required for extensive takes in these formats.

Most professional wildlife movies are made with 16mm film. The three standard brands of cameras in this format are Arriflex (German), Beaulieu (French), and Bolex (Swiss). Amateur movies were once made almost exclusively on standard 8mm film, which is really 16mm film exposed on one half its width, then reversed and exposed on the other half. In processing it is split and yields two strips of 8mm film. Recently, however, Super 8 film has achieved a remarkable popularity and there is no doubt that camera manufacturers are banking on Super 8 as the standard small format of the future. So many different Super 8 camera models are currently available, and new models are being introduced so rapidly, that it is impossible to recommend at this point the best model for our purposes. Obviously a model for wildlife photography should have through-the-lens viewing and automatic exposure adjustments. Either interchangeable lenses or a high-quality zoom lens is almost a necessity. Additionally, a heavy-duty power pack and the capability of using extra-long film footages are desirable. The camera should have variable speeds of from eight to sixty-four frames per second, and a film-footage indicator.

The movie photographer's approach to his work must be different from that of the still photographer. The still photographer most often strives to achieve a portrait—a nearly full-frame image of his quarry, frequently with the animal in an attitude of repose. The movie photographer, on the other hand, usually wants to show the animal's normal behavior in its environment and so must show a fairly large area of the animal's surroundings on each frame. He will, of course, want to include some closeups, but even these will probably be shot from a distance so as not to disturb or distract the animal. Few people enjoy looking at film of animals standing still and looking suspiciously in the direction of the camera.

Good movies tell a story, and there are two basic story structures that are stock in trade for wildlife films. The simplest to produce is a travelogue which tells the story of a journey and the animals seen along the way. The trip may be across Africa or around a small pond—actual distance is inconsequential and in fact the "trip" may be merely a convenient way of tying the various sequences to a common theme. The animals are usually photographed at a convenient control point where they are resting, feeding, or drinking. The photographer depends upon the mere image of the animals on the screen to provide visual interest and does not necessarily have to show exciting action, though of course he will if he can. Almost anyone with sufficient skill and patience can produce attractive wildlife films of this type.

The other major type of movie tells the story of some event in the life of one or perhaps many animals. Typical stories might center on a mated pair of animals rearing their young to maturity; a young animal learning to survive on its own; the social behavior of animals living in groups; an annual migration of animals; or some unusual (often fictional) adventure of one or more animals. Many such films require trained or semi-domesticated animals and several months of filming time. Stories such as these are staples of the Walt Disney studio, the National Geographic Society, and a few free-lancing professionals, such as Jacques Cousteau, who often obtain considerable financial backing for their enterprises. This type of movie almost demands professional standards because of the time and expense involved in producing them—and they sometimes yield handsome financial rewards.

Movie photography is typically conducted with the camera inside the blind, where the photographer controls the panning, focal length of the lens, film speed, and other important variables. Occasionally the camera may be mounted outside the blind, where it is aimed at a control point and operated from within the blind via a remote release cable.

ANIMAL RESPONSES TO PHOTOGRAPHIC EQUIPMENT

When a human goes stalking into an animal's territory, the animal will respond pretty much the same whether the intruder is carrying a camera or not. The animal will flee when it discovers a human within its safety zone. The stalker, then, has two alternatives: He can work from outside the animal's safety zone by using a long telephoto lens; or he can attempt to penetrate the animal's safety zone with the expectation that the animal will flee the first time the shutter is tripped and his presence is revealed.

A blind, however, creates a different situation. Once the photographer conceals himself inside, the animal can no longer see a human presence. It may respond to human sounds or smells, but these stimuli seem to be perceived by the animal as far less dangerous when a corresponding visual stimulus is absent. Still, some animals may be afraid of the blind itself, though others may not be. I put up a portable blind near a small pond in a marsh at the Virginia coast to photograph wading birds, and had scarcely got inside before a belted kingfisher and later an immature black-crowned night heron adopted the blind for a perch; but great egrets who used the pond as a feeding ground would only circle overhead and fly away, obviously reluctant to land at a favorite spot because they feared the blind. Again, I've seen a deer walk cautiously up to a blind and stick its nose against it, obviously curious, but another deer skittishly whiff it from a distance of twenty yards and then turn tail and run. Indeed, unless the blind is placed near a nest or den where family are being reared, an animal's responses to it are so unpredictable that most photographers quickly learn that they cannot know what to expect.

Probably most wildlife photography employing blinds is

Animal responses to photographic blinds are unpredictable. This immature night heron perched on my blind only moments after it had been erected. Yet the same blind aroused suspicion among other species of birds during the entire afternoon it was in place.

done at nests or dens containing young, for this is the time when the animal family centers the most activity in a small area. If relatively large mammals are being photographed—say a coyote family or a cougar mother and cubs—the blind will usually have to be situated some distance away and shooting conducted with a long telephoto lens because the animals are likely to be suspicious and fearful of the human scent around the blind. Large shy birds, such as some hawks and owls, are also likely to be disturbed by the mere presence of a blind if it is located too close to the nest. Most smaller mammals and birds, however, will accept the presence of a blind fairly close to the den or nest if it is properly introduced.

There are two ways to introduce a blind. One technique is to select the blind site and place on it a moderately small object such as a weighted cardboard box or a plastic pail. Many animals will apparently accept a small object much more readily than a blind; if the smaller object is accepted in a given spot, a day or so later it can be removed and replaced by a blind with very little disturbance to the animal. Another, more traditional technique is to move the blind into position in stages over a period of days. Three days is a standard time. On the first day the blind is erected some distance from the chosen site, placed in such a way that the animals will not fail to notice it but will not feel intimidated by its presence. The blind is left unoccupied. On the second day the blind is moved halfway to the chosen site and again left unoccupied, and on the third day it is placed in final position.

In all cases when blinds are introduced, the animals are observed from a distance to see if they accept the strange object and go about their ordinary routines. If after an hour or so they fail to accept the item, it should be removed a short distance and the animals given more time to get used to it. If this practice is not followed, the lives of the young, who need the constant attention of their parents, may be endangered. Some species of birds and mammals will allow a more rapid introduction of the blind—the entire process may be compressed into a few hours or even less. But never should a blind be intruded suddenly into the immediate area of the young; to do so is to frighten and disturb the entire family needlessly.

In almost any species there are individual animals that are so suspicious and fearful and so unnerved by the presence of a blind that they can never accept it no matter how carefully it is introduced. The photographer who encounters such a subject should pull up stakes and seek other quarry, for he is not going to get pictures and is clearly endangering the lives of the young.

A camera operated inside a blind will usually cause some disturbance among the animals when it is first used. The click of the shutter may cause birds to burst into flight and mammals to disappear into holes. But usually the recovery is quick, and after a brief reconnoiter the animals will return to their routines. The fear responses to the sounds of the camera will gradually diminish until the animals will finally ignore them altogether. In my experience, the sound of the shutter is less frightening to birds than a movement of a camera lens that protrudes outside the blind. If the lens must be moved to change its aim or focus, it should be moved very slowly, and if possible only when the bird is looking in another direction.

Cameras and lights mounted outside a blind and operated remotely should be introduced in the same way as the blind—gradually. When the blind is first erected some distance away, for example, a tripod might be set up near it. As the blind is moved forward, the tripod might also be moved, by gradual stages, into its final position. After it is clearly accepted, the light stands might be introduced one at a time, then the lights, and finally the camera. By then the blind should be in position and photographing can commence. At a bird nest it is preferable to take the first photograph immediately after the parents have finished feeding the young—not before—as this ensures that the first disturbance will not cause the young to miss a meal. The first time the camera trips and the lights flash the parent will start. Sometimes it will fly away, sometimes it will simply react with a quick flutter of its wings. In any case, it will be unsettled for a few minutes and will give some suspicious and perhaps hostile looks toward the equipment. It is highly desirable to let the parents feed the young several times without interruption before taking another picture. Most birds will display less and less response to subsequent picture taking, but there are always exceptions. I once photographed a yellow-breasted chat nest at which one bird (which I took to be the female because of her more subdued coloring) almost immediately lost all fear of the equipment, while the other never failed to panic when the camera fired. After three or four tries I stopped photographing the male and concentrated entirely on the female, and my work did not seem to interrupt the feeding of the young at all. I did not count my painstaking efforts at that nest a success, though, until the young had fledged, and that leads us to the next topic.

PHOTOGRAPHIC ETHICS

A wildlife photographer's primary concern should be the well-being of his subjects. This should take clear precedence over his getting good pictures, or for that matter any pictures at all. Any prolonged disturbance to young animals as a result of improperly introducing the blind and other equipment is inexcusable. Bird photographers are likely to have difficult problems around nests because of the vegetation in which most are concealed. If the vegetation is left in place it interferes with a clear portrait of the bird; if it is disturbed, the young are threatened by exposure to lethal rain, sunlight, or predation. A fairly safe rule is this: Concealing vegetation should never be cut away from a nest; it should be pulled back and tied while photographing takes place, and then should be allowed to spring back into place when the session is finished. Useful devices for holding back vegetation are half-inch-wide rubber strips cut from an old automobile inner tube—these are much easier to manage than bits of string—and common spring-loaded clothespins. Used carefully, neither will strip off leaves or otherwise damage vegetation. When a good photographer finishes his work and removes his equipment, there is hardly any evidence at all that he was there, and the nest and young are as well concealed as ever.

Photographers should also take precautions when working tree nests in wooded areas. A number of animals, notably the widely distributed raccoon, will follow a trail of human scent in hopes of scavenging. They will readily climb a tree that has a human scent on it, and bird banders, falconers, and others who study bird nests recommend that a metal shield be placed around the trunk of a nest tree that has been climbed. A piece of tin wrapped around the trunk and nailed into place will, if large enough, prevent the marauder from getting a foothold and will stop his progress upward.

It should go without saying that no one who is not part of a management program should attempt to photograph rare or endangered species during the reproductive cycle.

I strongly recommend that anyone who wishes to take up wildlife photography read Eliot Porter's *Birds of North America: A Personal Selection.* In it he describes his experiences during almost thirty years of serious bird photography and details the sometimes remarkable efforts he has made to safeguard the lives of his subjects. In that respect, as well as in the excellence of his photography, Porter's work serves as a model for us all.

XI

NAVIGATION

Several years ago a man driving his family along a Canadian highway parked his car on the shoulder of the road and went into the woods to relieve a physical need. He was never seen again, and evidence showed that he had simply wandered off in the wrong direction. I have been on birding walks with small parties and seen individuals get completely and utterly disoriented in a tract of woods no bigger than three acres. Every year dozens of hunters get lost in the woods, often in areas they have hunted in before. Why?

Probably most people get lost by trusting to what they call their "sense of direction." Unfortunately this so-called "sense" does not exist in humans, though it is found in some animals. Birds, for example, can actually sense the earth's magnetic field and thus have a true internal directional sense. But humans, at least as far as we know now, have not even a hint of an inner directional or navigational system. This was established by extensive experiments in which blindfolded subjects were asked to walk or drive a jeep in a straight line across a perfectly flat dry lake bed. The experiments were conducted on cloudy, windless days so that no directional clues would be available to the subjects from the environment. Invariably the blindfolded subjects traveled in circles, some circling to the left, others to the right. Similar results were obtained when they were blindfolded and asked to swim or paddle a boat across a body of water. Many of the subjects, when confronted with what they had done, refused to believe that they had not followed a straight line and claimed that the experiment had been rigged in some way to throw them off course; a few even became angry, insisting that they *had* followed a straight line. So much for the human's "sense of direction."

Even granting that we have no inner directional sense, why do we tend to follow a circular path across land or water? To date no adequate explanation has been offered. The "dominant side" theory was discarded after no correlation was found between the tendency to circle right or left and being right-handed and right-footed or left-handed and left-footed or any permutation of these. Neither is there any correlation between the tendency to circle in one direction and differences in leg length or muscular development. All we can say is that it appears each person has a tendency to circle either right or left, but as yet we don't know why.

When a person with a strong trust in his "sense of direction" happens to walk unknowingly in a circle, bizarre results sometimes emerge. There are numerous records of such individuals insisting that their compasses had begun to point in the wrong direction; some have insisted that rivers and streams were flowing backward; and a few have even argued that the sun was rising in the wrong place! Physical disorientation does strange things to the mind, and that is partly why it is so dangerous, for it can lead to a state of almost complete irrationality.

How do you avoid serious disorientation outdoors? Simply by recognizing that your inner "sense of direction" is about as reliable as a broken watch and relying instead on external reference points. The simplest way to keep your bearings, of course, is to stay on or close to a well-marked route of travel—a road, a trail, a path, a stream bed, a lake shore. Such an unmistakable route enables you to go into an area and come out again in almost any kind of weather, day or night. But if no well-marked route is available and travel must be cross-country, other kinds of reference points must be used.

First, let's talk about some kinds of references that should *not* be used. Probably everyone has heard the old adage about moss growing on the north side of a tree. Don't believe it. Moss grows on any side of a tree trunk with the right conditions of moisture and shade, and these conditions are determined by the canopy of the tree, the canopy of surrounding trees, the slope of the land, prevailing winds, and possibly other factors as well. Moss can grow just as well on the south side of a tree as on the north side, regardless of whether the tree is solitary or part of a larger stand of trees. Another questionable tale is that the bark and growth rings of a tree will be thickest on the north side. Maybe so, but in my experience, in addition to the hatchet or knife necessary to cut into the tree, you would have to be equipped with a vernier-scaled micrometer or a $10 \times$ magnifying loupe with reticle to tell the difference. It would be much simpler just to carry a compass. Another bit of folklore advises you to use the prevailing wind direction. The trick, of course, is determining when the wind is in its "prevailing" direction. Still other bits of advice tell you to look at the growth patterns of flowers, the openings of animal dens, and the colors of rocks. Now I am not saying that these adages do not contain a shred of truth and would never be reliable. But they are demonstrably unreliable in many instances and I would advise anyone faced with the necessity of determining directions to use more dependable guides. If you need to determine north-south directions you can use celestial reference points almost anywhere in the world. If you need to determine your position in regard to a topographical location, you can use terrestrial reference points. A topographic map and a compass will enable you to determine these things and much more with remarkable accuracy.

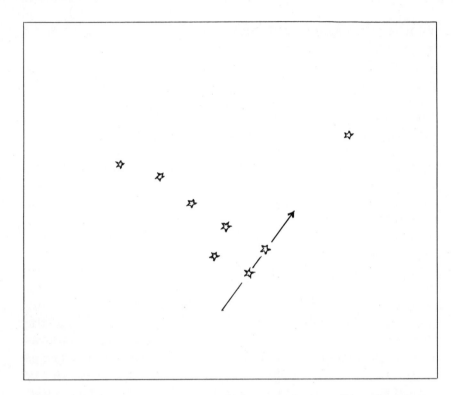

The Big Dipper rotates around the North Star, but the two pointer stars opposite the handle always point toward the North Star.

Undoubtedly the celestial reference point most commonly used by outdoorsmen is the sun, which as everyone knows rises approximately in the east and sets approximately in the west. When the sun is high above the horizon, however, most people have difficulty using it to determine direction. Here is a simple method. Push one end of a double-pointed stick into the ground so it casts a shadow. Carefully mark the spot where the tip of the shadow ends. Wait an hour or so and again carefully mark the tip of the shadow. Now draw a straight line through the two marks. This line will run approximately west-east. Another line drawn from the base of the stick perpendicular to this line will point approximately north (in the northern hemisphere). At night, most people can use the rising and setting of the moon and stars to determine direction, and most can also find the North Star by using the Big Dipper as a reference. The two stars forming the side of the cup away from the handle point to the North Star. Beginning at the star on the bottom of the cup, draw an imaginary line through the top star and extend it outward roughly six times the distance between the two cup stars. The line will end approximately on the bright North Star.

On most outings it is really not necessary to know compass directions—you need only know your position in relation to some fixed point on the topography. Make sure that your reference point is fixed, and do not make the mistake I once saw made by a young man from New Jersey. Three of us were hiking a remote trail in the Gallatin Forest in Montana. We had left the point of a hairpin turn in the forest trail and walked downhill to the edge of a large meadow, intending to examine a stream that ran through it. Since we would have to walk back uphill from precisely this point to find the trail easily and reliably, my companion, who was a Montana native, suggested that we mark the spot in some way. Our New Jersey companion looked briefly around. "Ah! I know," he said with the air of one who has complete confidence in his woodcraft. "There's a grizzly bear on the grassy slope on the far side of the meadow. Can you see it?" I squinted in the direction he was pointing and sure enough, there in the far distance was the unmistakable hulking form of a bear. "Well," said our companion, "the bear and the tip of that distant snowcapped mountain peak line up perfectly from here. All we have to do in coming back is to walk along the edge of the woods until the bear and the peak form a straight line, and we'll be exactly at this spot."

Sometimes sounds can be used as references—for example, the sound of a moving stream or a waterfall, of ocean surf, railway or highway traffic. The usefulness of sounds vanishes if you get too far away to hear them, or if there is more than one possible source for the sounds—two waterfalls, say, or two highways whose sounds might be confused.

Visible terrestrial reference points are undoubtedly the most convenient and widely used in simple walking. They can do almost anything, and in fact can be a combination of so many things that you're hard pressed to say exactly what you're using. My usual method of navigation takes into account sun position, but also makes use of the total appearance of the landscape as I move along: I notice the slope of the terrain, the direction of flow of streams, the shape of rock outcroppings, patterns of vegetation, unusual trees, etc. I also stop frequently and look back along my route to see what it looks like in reverse perspective. This system seems to work fine for me. When the sky is overcast, however, and I'm in strange or remote territory without a map or compass, I often leave a visible trail by scuffing the ground every few yards so I could backtrack myself out if necessary. This method can be used while stalking if you're careful about where and how you mark your trail.

There are numerous other methods more specific than visualizing the whole landscape. Which one works best is often dependent on the lay of the land. In rolling or mountainous country, for instance, it is often feasible to navigate by using terrain features. For example, if you walk down the crest of a ridge to its point, turn left across a stream, go up the next ridge to its crest, turn right and walk half a mile, then it's a simple matter to walk back the same way, using the features of the terrain as reference points. Terrain features can be used in very complex ways, but if the system becomes very elaborate, it's a good idea to make a written description or a simple map to help keep the details straight in your mind. One wrong turn is all you need to become helplessly disoriented.

In any kind of terrain, but especially in open, flat terrain, prominent reference points on the distant horizon are particularly useful. You could choose a mountain peak, a butte, a peculiar rock formation, a tall tree, a patch of snow or vegetation, perhaps a distant water tower or radio tower with a blinking light on top, especially useful if circumstances should keep you out until darkness falls. After dark, the glow of town or city lights can be seen from a great distance even during overcast weather.

A magnetic compass, of course, provides an excellent reference point because it usually points faithfully toward the earth's north magnetic pole. I say "usually" because a compass can be fooled, and it can fool you. A compass needle can be pulled away from magnetic north by nearby metal objects—an automobile, a power line, a gun, even a watch or a knife. To ensure an accurate reading, always stand at least twenty feet away from a power line or automobile, ten or so from a gun, and keep the compass an arm's length away from knives and other metal objects you might be carrying. Further, diligently avoid putting your compass close to operating electric motors, including the starter on your car. Close exposure to these may

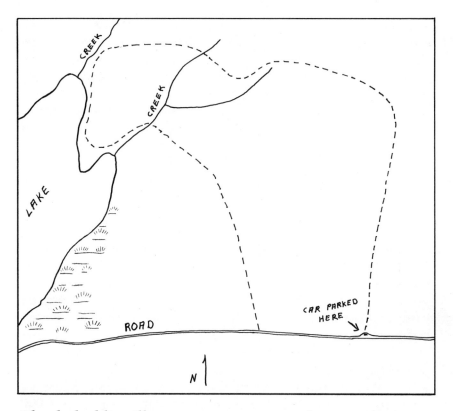

The dashed line illustrates a return route that was intentionally diverted so as to encounter the road to the west of the parked car. The traveller can then be sure he can find his car by walking east along the road. The same technique can be used along streams, lake shores, etc., to find camps or other points with a minimum of effort.

cause the compass needle to reverse polarity and point not at the north magnetic pole, but directly away from it! If this happens and you're not aware of it, you could be in for some real trouble. Whenever you go out with a compass it's a good idea to check it first in an area where you are sure of the directions, just to be safe.

If you wish to start from a road or trail and walk cross-country on a circular route back to your road or trail, you might want to use the technique of following an intentionally diverted route. Here's how it works. Suppose you're on a road that runs east-west through a large forest; you want to park your car and walk a circular route to the north. If you try to come back onto the road exactly where you parked your car, the chances are that you will miss it and the car will not be in sight. Which way do you go to find it—east or west? You really don't know unless you can see tire tracks (or lack of them), but this may not be possible. However, there will be no problem at all if, while walking, you use your reference points to intentionally direct your return route to the west of your parked car. Then when you come to the road you will know that your car is to the east and you can go directly to it without wasting time or effort.

Following a diverted return route is usually not necessary if you're using the most sophisticated of all manual navigational techniques, that of orienting yourself with the aid of a map and compass. With a good topographic map (ordinary road maps are useless for such work) and an accurate compass you can locate yourself to within a few feet on the terrain by one or more means. Map-and-compass navigation is recommended for anyone going very far afield in unfamiliar terrain. An excellent discussion of this type of navigation is found in Bjorn Kjellstrom's interesting book, *Be Expert with Map and Compass*. Copies can be found in most stores that sell books on outdoor subjects.

Topographic maps for the United States are available in a few outdoor-supply stores, or they may be ordered directly from the government agencies which prepare them. If ordering from the government you should initially request an order form, specifying the states and counties for which you wish maps. The order forms are free; maps sell for a modest price. For maps covering areas east of the Mississippi write: Distribution Section, USGS, 1200 S. Eads St., Arlington, Va. 22202. For maps west of the Mississippi write: Distribution Section, USGS, Federal Center, Denver, Colo. 80225. For Alaska write: USGS, 520 Illinois Street, Fairbanks, Alaska. Canadian topographic maps may be ordered from: Map Distribution Office, Department of Mines and Technical Surveys, 615 Booth Street, Ottawa, Ontario, Canada.

A word of caution is, I hope, needless. If you plan to navigate by map and compass, learn the basic techniques *before* you go out into the wilderness and face a serious navigational problem. Also, do not attempt to learn without a good book or an experienced person as a guide. In using topographic maps you must learn to deal with a little devil known as magnetic declination, which is the difference between the earth's north rotational pole and its north magnetic pole. Correcting for the difference is particularly tricky because the magnetic pole tends to drift from year to year. Topographic maps are marked with grid lines which run east-west and north-south in accordance with the earth's rotational poles; but magnetic north rarely coincides with these map lines and may depart from them by many degrees on the compass. Without a thorough knowledge of how to use declination correctly, you can use a map and compass and get more convincingly lost than you might without them. Using them correctly, however, you can determine not only where you are in relation to a given point, but also the most desirable route to get you there, whether for ease of walking, or concealment, or almost any other goal you may have.

XII

TRACKING

Most of this book has been concerned with how to get close to wild animals for whatever purposes the individual desires—simple observation, photography, or hunting. This chapter is written principally for hunters and is concerned with the special skills a hunter needs when he has had the unfortunate experience of wounding a quarry that manages to escape.

In such circumstances a hunter has a moral obligation to track the animal until he can bring it down or until he is satisfied that the wound is only superficial. Though some of the techniques discussed here can be used to track uninjured game, they are oriented primarily toward the pursuit of wounded quarry.

Perhaps the first thing we need to do is to attack the mystique of tracking. Almost everyone in our culture is familiar with a stock character from movies and novels about the American frontier. He is frequently known simply as a "tracker" and is often presented as aloof, silent, and mysterious, but he can sit on a horse for days on end through the unholiest of terrain in pursuit of renegades. Every so often he stops to look at the ground and then points infallibly in the direction the outlaws traveled, while ordinary mortals riding with him look at the same piece of ground and see absolutely nothing. In one recent movie, such a man successfully tracked the lawbreakers even though they followed a devilishly twisting route across miles of bare rock! As portrayed in our legends and art forms, the skills of tracking seem astounding and inexplicable, like the skills of mindreading or divination.

Now, mind you, there really are people who can perform seemingly incredible feats of tracking. But while their skills may seem uncanny to the ordinary person, in fact they are not mysterious at all and certainly do not partake of the supernatural. The best trackers are people of great natural ability who have undergone a long and rigorous discipline in the wild. They have acquired a minute familiarity with the appearance of terrain, an eye for the tiniest of details, and a thorough familiarity with the nature and habits of their quarry. Such knowledge is acquired only by those who have lived in the wild for months on end. But this rare kind of refinement of tracking skills is not essential to tracking a wounded deer, which requires skills of a different order and can be accomplished by almost anyone with good eyesight, patience, and the ability to employ a commonsense method.

Let's begin at the critical moment when the shot is released and the quarry begins moving away, usually at a run. Your first thought should be to stay exactly where you are and get a visual fix on the spot where the quarry stood when the shot was released and the line followed by the animal when it began running. If you move before you get this fix, your visual perspective will change and you may spend a long, frustrating time looking in the wrong place for the trail.

With this fix firmly established in mind, your next step should be to recall your sight picture at the moment the shot was released, along with the pattern of recoil. Were the sights correctly aligned? Was the aim perhaps high or low or to one side, or possibly into a tree or bush? If the shot connected would it have been in the head, chest, abdomen—or where? This information is crucial in determining whether, or where, the quarry may be wounded and possibly the type and severity of the wound. Also, what did the recoil feel like? Did it feel normal, solid, and straight back into the shoulder? Or was the gun poorly supported and did this cause the recoil to jump in an unusual direction? If the ammunition being used has a slow barrel time, an unusual angle-of-jump during recoil can throw the point of impact completely off target. Finally, recall the animal's response the instant after the shot was fired. Did it stagger or in some way appear to be hit, or did it begin its escape strongly and smoothly, as if unhit? These and perhaps other clues can be found in your visual memory of releasing the shot and can be invaluable in helping you later to analyze evidence found on the animal's trail.

If you believe the animal to be hit, then you should go directly to the spot where it stood and establish a reference point by noting your relation to an easily identifiable tree, rock, or other landmark, or by marking the spot with a hat or some other object. Immediately sight along the path the animal followed as it fled. With reasonably good luck in the condition of the ground cover, you should be able to see at least one set of track marks left by the animal's feet. We'll come back to the question of how to look for these marks later; for the moment, just assume that you can see them. Now, without changing your position, look beyond the first set of marks and try to find the second, third, and so on, for as far as you can see. If you have binoculars, they will provide an excellent way of examining the ground for as much as twenty yards ahead. Get a firm mental fix on the trail for as far as you can. Memorize it and take a second look at the tracks before you move.

Now you can begin moving about in search of evidence of a wound. If you fired a gun, look for signs of where the projectile(s) hit. Did they end up in tree trunks on the near side of your quarry? Then you can forget about a wounded animal. But you may find tufts of hair or spots of blood on the ground. Then you *must* track. You must also track if you cannot find any evidence at all of where the projectile hit, for sometimes a lethal wound does not bleed freely, particularly at first. In either case, you begin by proceeding along the trail as far as you have already identified it, being cautious about two things. First, you are careful not to obliterate the trail. Second, you walk crouched over, close to the ground, searching the ground cover with minute care to look for blood. You may wish to search on hands and knees. If you find blood, examine it carefully. Is it bright-red, arterial blood? Then the wound is probably lethal. Is it dark, veinous blood? If in small quantities, it may indicate a superficial wound, but don't make that judgment yet. Is the blood frothy? It indicates a lethal lung wound. Does it contain bits of bone? This is usually a sign of serious injury.

You now continue to move forward along the trail, searching primarily for blood, but also for other signs of injury—staggering or faltering patterns in the tracks. As you proceed, the first cardinal rule is this: *Always try to identify the trail in front of you before you move ahead.* This will seem tedious and your patience will be strained in this, but in the long run it will save you a great deal of time. Of course, it is not always possible to identify the next markings of the trail, because most trails do become invisible for short distances. So you will be forced to move ahead of your last identified mark, and the second cardinal rule is this: *Never leave the last sign of a trail without marking it so you can return directly to it.* If the last signs are footprints, examine them carefully. In which direction do they point? That's the direction you should go in search of your next set of marks. If you go in that direction and search unsuccessfully, return to the marked spot and think the situation through. How has the animal been moving thus far? Has it been working for speed moving through fairly open terrain? Or has it appeared to falter and might it be looking for thick cover and concealment? Try to think like your quarry and second-guess its next move. Sometimes this works. Using your best judgment, start searching carefully for the next trail signs, circling slowly in the best areas. Always keep the location of the last sign clearly identified, however, so you can return to it without losing the trail altogether and having to spend frustrating minutes or hours searching for the part of the trail you've already identified.

Essentially, these are the basic techniques of tracking wounded quarry. Emphasis is placed upon keeping the known part of the trail firmly in mind and searching systematically and methodically for the unknown part. The work is fairly simple, but it does require patience; and circumstances, particularly the nature of the ground cover, can make or break the success of tracking efforts. But it is rare indeed that a wounded animal can disappear without leaving some kind of detectable trail, even if it's only blood spoor. Let's consider now some of the ways of "reading" the blood spoor along a trail.

Say you've wounded a deer and have tracked it 200 yards or more. The distance between the tracks reveals that the animal is not slowing down, and the blood spoors, which are dark red, appear to be diminishing. What should you do? Consider carefully: You've probably got an animal with a nonlethal wound. A fresh bullet wound is anesthetized by the shock of the bullet's impact, but as sensation returns after an hour or so the animal is going to feel pain. There is also some risk of infection occurring in the wound. In short, you should make every reasonable effort to track the animal down, being prepared to have to shoot again from a considerable distance. If you get the opportunity for a second shot, make it count. Figure out what your mistake was on the first shot, take your time, and bring the animal down cleanly.

Again, suppose you've tracked your quarry about 200 yards and though you can't tell for sure whether it's slowing down, you continue to find a heavy arterial blood spoor. Keep going. The animal is not only going to suffer, it is going to die. If you leave it in that condition, you are no sportsman, you haven't the morals for it, and you should abdicate the right to hunt. This holds true in the case of any kind of evidence you find of a seriously wounded quarry. You have to keep going until darkness stops you, and the next day you have to come back and keep going, praying in the meantime that it doesn't rain and wash away the trail. The work may be difficult and tedious, but you've got to try. Fortunately, if the quarry is seriously wounded, your tracking efforts are likely to end in success in a reasonably short time. Almost by definition, a seriously wounded animal does not travel very far.

There are three dangers you encounter in tracking. The first, as ridiculous as it sounds, is that you can get yourself lost. Don't look just at the ground; glance up and around occasionally to keep yourself visually oriented to the terrain features. You may want to mark your own trail with scuff marks on the ground so you can easily backtrack out. The second danger is that you can easily get shot by other hunters. Wearing blaze orange is one of the best preventive measures. Even if you don't wear it ordinarily while hunting, carry a lightweight blaze-orange vest in your pocket and wear it while tracking. The third danger is in getting too close to a wounded quarry that has become vicious. Often it will appear to be dead, and in fact may be unconscious, but your presence will serve as a stimulus to revive it, along with its fear and rage. Assume the animal is dangerous until you have determined absolutely that it's dead.

Ground clues in tracking

If you're tracking your quarry across a ground cover of snow, mud, or some other impressionable surface, or even through wet vegetation, you'll likely have little or no trouble following the trail because it should be highly visible even at a distance. A leaf-covered forest floor usually does not present much of a problem if the animal has hoofed feet, is heavy, and is moving rapidly. Under such conditions the leaf cover will be visibly disturbed, and hoofprints in the soil beneath the leaves can be verified by running the fingers over the surface of the ground. If the animal has padded feet, however, the signs are going to be less visible and greater skill and patience will be required. Rock also presents a problem, but it's seldom that one comes upon a rock surface that is unbroken for any great distance. Careful searching usually finds the trail where it emerges from the rock onto impressionable ground again.

Your ability to see ground clues on a leaf-covered forest floor will improve with practice. If you'd like to work on developing this skill, here's a simple way to start. Take a piece of scrap wood somewhat larger than your forearm and stud it liberally with heavy nails so that the nails protrude about one inch above the surface. Tie about fifteen feet of cord to this and have a friend drag it through the woods from a known starting point but along an unknown route. The device should pull up enough leaves to leave a visible trail, but one that is subtle enough to pose some challenge to your powers of observation. At first you may have some difficulty seeing the trail, but as you study the forest floor you will soon learn to differentiate between a disturbed and an undisturbed leaf cover. When you can easily

A running deer or other heavy animal usually leaves highly visible tracks on at least parts of its course. These indicate the general direction of travel and aid the tracker in locating the more concealed footprints that require careful searching.

follow the trail of your friend pulling this device, try tracking him without it. He should begin by shuffling his feet to make his trail a bit more visible, then gradually reduce the shuffling until he is walking normally. If your powers of observation are good, in time you'll progress to being able to see where animals have walked along the forest floor. You may stand and point along such a trail, which seems perfectly clear to you, while your buddy stands and looks and professes to see nothing. Then you may be embarrassed to discover that you have difficulty expressing in words just what you see or how you see it. You know the trail is there, but you can't convey to others how you know. This can become a troublesome situation if your buddies start ribbing you about being able to see "invisible" trails. But then one day perhaps you'll have an opportunity to track down a wounded quarry for them. This may impress them with your skill, but more important, it may impress upon them that in hunting, sportsmanship and woodcraft are intimately intertwined. Truly sportsmanlike hunters do not attempt to overmatch a quarry with enormous firepower, but rather to pit woodcraft and hunting skills against a quarry in such a way that the animal has at least an even chance and is pursued with honesty and respect. This level of sportsmanship can be attained solely by an individual who has an intimate acquaintance not only with details of his quarry's behavior and appearance, but also with the details of the environment it inhabits—the trees, ground cover, plants, birds, mammals, reptiles, even the soils and water tables. A truly sportsmanlike hunter is not only an excellent shot—he is a skilled woodsman and a well-rounded naturalist who can go into a woodland with or without a gun and, either way, feel intense interest and pleasure in his association with nature.

BIBLIOGRAPHY:
SUGGESTIONS FOR FURTHER READING

FIELD GUIDES

Books. Birders will want to own the guide to field identification by Chandler Robbins *et al., Birds of North America* in the Golden Field Guide Series; and one or more of Roger Tory Peterson's *A Field Guide to the Birds* (Eastern United States), *A Field Guide to Western Birds,* and *A Field Guide to the Birds of Texas and Adjacent States* in the Peterson Field Guide Series. Those interested in mammals will want *A Field Guide to the Mammals* and possibly *A Field Guide to Animal Tracks* from the Peterson series. As interests expand, the Peterson series includes volumes on North American wild flowers (one volume covering the northeastern and north-central states, one covering the Rocky Mountains), ferns, trees and shrubs, rocks and minerals, butterflies, insects, bird nests, reptiles and amphibians, seashells (one volume for the Atlantic Coast, one for the Pacific Coast), and stars and planets. Other volumes in the series cover the birds of Mexico, birds of Britain and Europe, and mammals of Britain and Europe. The Golden Field Guide Series also includes volumes on the seashells of North America and the trees of North America. Many other field guides are available on a variety of subjects in North America as well as other regions.

Records. Recorded bird songs keyed to the Peterson Field Guide books have been produced by the Cornell Laboratory of Ornithology. The laboratory has also produced records of the songs of selected groups of birds, insect calls, frog calls, and the natural sounds of various local areas. The Federation of Ontario Naturalists has produced useful records of the calls of the finches, the warblers, the thrushes, the wrens, and the mockingbirds of eastern North America. Records of bird sounds are also included in the National Geographic Society's two-volume set of books, *Song and Garden Birds of North America* and *Water, Prey, and Game Birds of North America.*

Where to buy field guides

Many bookstores carry field guides. However, by purchasing your nature books, records, art prints, jewelry, and other items from the following two organizations you help support their conservation and research efforts. Members also frequently receive discounts.

Cornell Laboratory of Ornithology
159 Sapsucker Woods Road
Ithaca, N.Y. 14853

National Wildlife Federation
1412 Sixteenth Street N.W.
Washington, D.C. 20036

A wide range of books (including Bent's *Life Histories of North American Birds*), records, and other materials of interest to the naturalist are available from a private firm:

The Audubon Bookcase
3890 Stewart Road
Eugene, Ore. 97402

All three sources will supply a catalog upon request.

PHOTOGRAPHY

Information on almost every aspect of photography can be found in Eastman Kodak publications. In-stock titles are listed annually in a pamphlet, *Index to Kodak Information*, available in most camera stores or from Eastman Kodak Company, Department 454, 343 State Street, Rochester, N.Y. 14650. Those interested in nature photography will find useful information on films in two booklets, *Kodak Color Films* and *Kodak Professional Black-and-White Films*. Anyone interested in view-camera operations and techniques should read *Photography with Large Format Cameras*. A number of publications are available on movie making.

Excellent books dealing with nature photography are *Photographing Nature* in the Life Library of Photography series, and *Wildlife Photography: A Field Guide* by Eric Hosking and John Gooders (New York: Praeger, 1973). Also of interest is *Photographing Wildlife* by J. M. Baufle and J. P. Varin, originally in French, translated by Carel V. Amerongen (New York: Oxford University Press, 1972). The serious bird photographer will want to read Eliot Porter's *Birds of North America: A Personal Selection* (New York: E. P. Dutton, 1974) both for its photographs and its text.

ADDITIONAL READING

The National Geographic Society publishes a number of titles of interest to the naturalist. A catalog can be obtained by writing the National Geographic Society, Washington, D.C. 20036. Recommended: *The Marvels of Animal Behavior*, which gives fascinating accounts of a number of animals throughout the world; and *Song and Garden Birds of North America* and *Water, Prey, and Game Birds of North America*, a two-volume set, thoroughly illustrated, describing the birds found in North America north of Mexico.

The Life Nature Library contains a number of fascinating, lavishly illustrated volumes. Of special interest perhaps are Roger Tory Peterson's volume *The Birds*, and Richard Carrington's volume *The Mammals*. Copies are available in most libraries and bookstores, or may be ordered through most bookstores.

The study of birds has become so popular and so much is being written about them that a seriously interested layman or student may be at a loss over what to read. One of the best current ornithology texts is Joel Carl Welty's *The Life of Birds*, second edition (Philadelphia: W. B. Saunders Company, 1975). Also of interest are G. J. Wallace's *An Introduction to Ornithology* (New York: Macmillan, 1955), and O. S. Pettingill's *Ornithology in Laboratory and Field* (Minneapolis: Burgess, 1970).

INDEX